DISCUSSION DRAFT, H.R. ____, "PUERTO RICO OVERSIGHT, MANAGEMENT, AND ECONOMIC STABILITY ACT (PROMESA)"

LEGISLATIVE HEARING

BEFORE THE

COMMITTEE ON NATURAL RESOURCES U.S. HOUSE OF REPRESENTATIVES

ONE HUNDRED FOURTEENTH CONGRESS

SECOND SESSION

Wednesday, April 13, 2016

Serial No. 114–36

Printed for the use of the Committee on Natural Resources

Available via the World Wide Web: http://www.fdsys.gov
or
Committee address: http://naturalresources.house.gov

U.S. GOVERNMENT PUBLISHING OFFICE

99–800 PDF   WASHINGTON : 2016

For sale by the Superintendent of Documents, U.S. Government Publishing Office
Internet: bookstore.gpo.gov Phone: toll free (866) 512–1800; DC area (202) 512–1800
Fax: (202) 512–2104 Mail: Stop IDCC, Washington, DC 20402–0001

COMMITTEE ON NATURAL RESOURCES

ROB BISHOP, UT, *Chairman*
RAÚL M. GRIJALVA, AZ, *Ranking Democratic Member*

Don Young, AK
Louie Gohmert, TX
Doug Lamborn, CO
Robert J. Wittman, VA
John Fleming, LA
Tom McClintock, CA
Glenn Thompson, PA
Cynthia M. Lummis, WY
Dan Benishek, MI
Jeff Duncan, SC
Paul A. Gosar, AZ
Raúl R. Labrador, ID
Doug LaMalfa, CA
Jeff Denham, CA
Paul Cook, CA
Bruce Westerman, AR
Garret Graves, LA
Dan Newhouse, WA
Ryan K. Zinke, MT
Jody B. Hice, GA
Aumua Amata Coleman Radewagen, AS
Thomas MacArthur, NJ
Alexander X. Mooney, WV
Cresent Hardy, NV
Darin LaHood, IL

Grace F. Napolitano, CA
Madeleine Z. Bordallo, GU
Jim Costa, CA
Gregorio Kilili Camacho Sablan, CNMI
Niki Tsongas, MA
Pedro R. Pierluisi, PR
Jared Huffman, CA
Raul Ruiz, CA
Alan S. Lowenthal, CA
Matt Cartwright, PA
Donald S. Beyer, Jr., VA
Norma J. Torres, CA
Debbie Dingell, MI
Ruben Gallego, AZ
Lois Capps, CA
Jared Polis, CO
Wm. Lacy Clay, MO

Jason Knox, *Chief of Staff*
Lisa Pittman, *Chief Counsel*
David Watkins, *Democratic Staff Director*
Sarah Lim, *Democratic Chief Counsel*

————

CONTENTS

LEGISLATIVE HEARING ON DISCUSSION DRAFT, H.R. ____, "PUERTO RICO OVERSIGHT, MANAGEMENT, AND ECONOMIC STABILITY ACT (PROMESA)"

Wednesday, April 13, 2016
U.S. House of Representatives
Committee on Natural Resources
Washington, DC

The committee met, pursuant to call, at 10:09 a.m., in room 1324, Longworth House Office Building, Hon. Rob Bishop [Chairman of the Committee] presiding.

Present: Representatives Bishop, Gohmert, Lamborn, Wittman, Fleming, McClintock, Benishek, Duncan, Gosar, Labrador, LaMalfa, Denham, Cook, Wasterman, Graves, Newhouse, Hice, Radewagen, MacArthur, Mooney, Hardy, LaHood, Grijalva, Bordallo, Costa, Tsongas, Pierluisi, Huffman, Ruiz, Lowenthal, Cartwright, Beyer, Torres, Dingell, Gallego, Polis, and Clay.

Also Present: Representatives Velazquez, Serrano, and Gutierrez.

The CHAIRMAN. The committee is going to be in order. We are meeting today to hear testimony on the discussion draft of the Puerto Rico Oversight, Management, and Economic Stability Act.

Under Committee Rule 4(f), oral opening statements are limited to the Chair, the Ranking Member, the Vice Chair, and the designee of the Ranking Member. I am going to ask unanimous consent that other Members' opening statements be made part of the hearing record if they are submitted to the Clerk by 5 p.m. today.

Hearing no objection, so ordered.

I also ask unanimous consent that Mr. Serrano, Ms. Velazquez, and Mr. Gutierrez, if they appear, be allowed to sit on the dais, and also Mr. Duffy as well.

Hearing no objection, so ordered.

I will also now excuse Mr. Duffy, who is a key player in this, obviously—he is going to be the sponsor of the legislation—who wished to be here, but he is also chairing another subcommittee at this very moment. So, because of that conflict, he is not going to be able to join us here now.

I now recognize myself, if I could, for a brief opening statement.

STATEMENT OF THE HON. ROB BISHOP, A REPRESENTATIVE IN CONGRESS FROM THE STATE OF UTAH

The CHAIRMAN. In the past couple of months, this committee has held multiple oversight hearings on this particular issue. This will be the fourth committee meeting we have had on testimony related to the situation in Puerto Rico, which is a whole lot of hearings. If you add them end to end, we would have enough video of just these hearings for a good daytime soap opera. We would give "Days

(1)

of Our Lives" a run for the money on the longest running daytime soap. And it would be just as riveting as those shows are, as well.

But the issue that is facing us has been basically decades in the making. There is over $118 billion in debt from bonds and pension liabilities that are there. Puerto Rico has not had an audited financial statement for 2 years. They are already in default on portions of their debt. We have to do something different.

Without the tools to ensure implementation of extensive government and economic reforms, Puerto Rico will continue to be on the cusp of default and run the risk of future calls for financial assistance or bailouts.

This bill includes reforms that can begin transitioning the island away from elements of cronyism, allow for privatization of an energy sector, and boost domestic activity that will be not only a short-term solution to the situation but also provide the island the tools to revitalize their economy in the long-term solution of it.

The Brookings Institute's Barry Bosworth recently said, "When you can't pay, you can't argue with the terms that much." Well, unfortunately, that is where we have come to. The United States needs to create a mode of strong oversight and reform in Puerto Rico's system, in which the government has grown simply too big, the debts are out of control, and the people are subject to overregulation. Enough is enough.

Some have proposed massive Federal spending and bailouts. This is simply a nonstarter and would pile on top of the problems that have led to Puerto Rico's current financial fiscal woes.

Others have sought to prioritize one group of creditors over another. That is a nonstarter. This bill protects existing creditor-to-debtor and creditor-to-creditor relationships according to existing law and the Constitution. And it fosters some much-needed change to move Puerto Rico toward economic freedom, privatization, and prosperity, while at the same time protecting taxpayers.

So, once again, let me emphasize, this is not going to be a bailout. This is going to be an effort to try and establish something based on precedents that have happened in the past to control the economic situation that is currently there. But, also, it is significant that within this bill are elements to try and provide economic viability going to the future. There has to be a way of making sure this problem does not come up over and over again.

I think what we have done over the years—I mean, this is also a unique process that we have tried to evolve in this particular bill. This is, as I said, the fourth public hearing we have had only on Puerto Rico. That is unusual. They have sent out two discussion drafts so that people could look at them and respond, which is unusual. We have tried to make sure that we do this not behind closed doors but out in public. We have received a whole bunch of recommendations from all sorts of different groups and have tried to incorporate as many as possible, I think most of them in this particular bill. I think we have done a good job. This is a good bill.

I look forward to hearing the testimony from the distinguished panel that we have here, and I appreciate you taking the time to join us today.

[The prepared statement of Mr. Bishop follows:]

PREPARED STATEMENT OF THE HON. ROB BISHOP, CHAIRMAN, COMMITTEE ON NATURAL RESOURCES

For the past few months, the committee has held three oversight hearings and received testimony from a variety of stakeholders relating to Puerto Rico. Today, the committee will review legislation to begin addressing the deepening fiscal crisis in Puerto Rico. This situation is the result of decades of mismanagement and a state-run economy destined for failure. With over *$118 billion in debt* in the form of bonds and unfunded pension liabilities, Puerto Rico has not produced audited financial statements for 2 years and has already defaulted on portions of its debt.

The situation will become much worse when Puerto Rico fails to make debt payments in less than a month. Large-scale defaults will occur, impacting millions of Americans both in Puerto Rico and on the mainland. Unfortunately, because the situation has gotten so dire, broad reforms are required *now*. Without tools to ensure transparency and implementation of extensive government and economic reforms, Puerto Rico will continue on the cusp of default and run the risk of future calls for a financial bailout.

This legislation eliminates that risk by creating a strong, independent oversight board to ensure needed reforms are carried out. The Board will be empowered to audit the Puerto Rican government and its corporations to see what's on the books and identify needed reforms and efficiencies. This will greatly aid with ongoing voluntary debt restructuring.

The bill includes reforms to begin transitioning the Island away from decades of state-run cronyism—allowing for privatization of its energy sector and a boost to domestic economic activity.

Let me be very clear of what this bill is not. It is *not* Chapter 9—a tool designed specifically by statute for municipalities of sovereign states. Puerto Rico is a U.S. *territory*. This bill is also *not* "Super" Chapter 9. To the contrary, it would ensure that no such dangerous precedent is set for states or in municipal bond markets by addressing the unique legal status of territories.

Certain groups are irresponsibly and falsely claiming that this bill is a bailout of Puerto Rico, which I vigorously oppose. Nothing could be further from the truth. This bill protects taxpayers by ensuring *not one dime* of taxpayer money is used to pay Puerto Rico's debt or otherwise bailout its government.

Recently, Brooking Institution economist Barry Bosworth said "when you can't pay, you can't argue over the terms that much." Unfortunately, it has come to that: the United States needs to create a mode of strong oversight and reform to rein in Puerto Rico's system in which the government has grown too big, the debts are out of control, and its people are subject to over-regulation and cronyism. Enough is enough.

Some have proposed massive new Federal spending. This is simply a non-starter and would pile on top of the problems that have led to Puerto Rico's current fiscal woes. Others have sought to prioritize one group of creditors over another. This is also a non-starter.

This bill protects existing creditor-to-debtor and creditor-to-creditor relationships according to existing law and the United States Constitution. It fosters much needed changes to move Puerto Rico toward economic freedom, privatization and prosperity, while at the same time protecting taxpayers.

It is a good bill and I look forward to hearing testimony from the distinguished panel here today.

———

The CHAIRMAN. With that, I will recognize Mr. Grijalva if he has an opening statement.

STATEMENT OF THE HON. RAÚL M. GRIJALVA, A REPRESENTATIVE IN CONGRESS FROM THE STATE OF ARIZONA

Mr. GRIJALVA. Thank you, Mr. Chairman.

Today, we are continuing the process toward passing legislation to help the people of Puerto Rico deal with a humanitarian crisis because of over $70 billion in unpayable debt.

It is worth stressing that we are here because the people of Puerto Rico need our help. Residents of Puerto Rico are struggling to receive basic services, with some hospitals now quite literally in the dark. On top of that, the Zika virus continues to ravage the island. Officials at the Centers for Disease Control and Prevention recently stated that they are quite concerned about the U.S. territory and tourist designation of Puerto Rico, stressing that one out of every four in Puerto Rico could host the Zika virus within a year.

In the meantime, wealthy Wall Street hedge funds that hold Puerto Rican bonds are spending millions of dollars to spread misinformation in an effort to block congressional action. These vulture funds are now aggressively campaigning against a solution to help the island relieve its debt. They are more interested in padding their profits than ensuring the well-being of American families suffering in Puerto Rico.

As Members of Congress, we have to decide tomorrow who comes first: vulture funds and others who steadfastly refuse to join other investors in good faith on a compromised solution or the American people in Puerto Rico.

The leadership of the House, Republicans and Democrats, has been working with Chairman Bishop and the Treasury Department to develop legislation that we can all support to provide Puerto Rico with the tools that they will need to solve this crisis.

Today, we are discussing the results of these bipartisan discussions, and we are all hopeful that the bill, as proposed, will work. To quote Secretary of Treasury, Jack Lew, "The question to us is, does the bill's restructuring authority work? It has to work, or it is not going to be acceptable." This will be one of the key questions we will look to our distinguished panel of witnesses to answer.

While the bill contains a strong oversight board to ensure that Puerto Rico will make the tough decisions to get on a path of a balanced budget and sound fiscal practices, there are a number of other concerns we have with the bill and the process.

We continue to insist that the oversight board should not impose further austerity, which will be counterproductive toward efforts to restore the island's economy.

We question the merit of authorizing a transfer of thousands of acres of the Vieques National Wildlife Refuge away from all the American people.

We also stress, as the Treasury Department does, that Puerto Rico will be unable to make any fiscal plan work going forward without the Medicaid support that is called for in the Treasury proposal and that such assistance be provided to smaller territories, as well. Puerto Rico's underfunded pensions should not be raided to help pay the debt, and the pensioners must be made whole.

We cannot see the logic behind lowering the minimum wage to $4.25 an hour for the very group of people we need to stay on the island in order to anchor this recovery.

Mr. Chairman, you and your staff deserve to be commended for your willingness to work in an honest and open process to address the crisis in Puerto Rico. To that end, I remain hopeful that we will be able to pass a bill out of committee tomorrow that will enjoy the support of all members, and I continue to pledge to work with you to realize that goal.

The people of Puerto Rico deserve no less, and the effort on their behalf should be constant with the perspective that I think is needed in this discussion: something that will help the people of Puerto

Rico and not something that will satisfy a particular political agenda or be the vehicle to assure that the vulture fund holders receive their full reimbursement that they are holding out for.

With that, I yield back and thank you, Mr. Chairman.

[The prepared statement of Mr. Grijalva follows:]

PREPARED STATEMENT OF THE HON. RAÚL M. GRIJALVA, RANKING MEMBER, COMMITTEE ON NATURAL RESOURCES

Thank you Mr. Chairman. Today we are continuing the process toward passing legislation to help the people of Puerto Rico deal with a humanitarian crisis because of over $70 billion in unpayable debt.

It is worth stressing that we are here because the people of Puerto Rico need our help! Residents of Puerto Rico are struggling to receive basic services, with some hospitals now quite literally in the dark. On top of this, the Zika virus continues to ravage the island. Officials at the Centers for Disease Control and Prevention (CDC) recently stated that they are "quite concerned" about the U.S. territory and tourist destination Puerto Rico, stressing that one out of every four people in Puerto could host the Zika virus within a year.

In the meantime, wealthy Wall Street hedge funds that hold Puerto Rican bonds are spending millions of dollars to spread misinformation in an effort to block congressional action. These vulture funds are now aggressively campaigning against a solution to help the island relieve some of its debt. They are more interested in padding their profits than ensuring the well-being of American families suffering in Puerto Rico.

As Members of Congress, we have to decide tomorrow who comes first—vulture funds and others who steadfastly refuse to join other investors in a good faith, compromise solution, or, the American people in Puerto Rico.

The leadership of the House—Republicans and Democrats—has been working with Chairman Bishop and the Treasury Department to develop legislation that we can all support to provide Puerto Rico with the tools they will need to solve the crisis.

Today we will be discussing the result of these bipartisan discussions and we are all hopeful that the bill as proposed will work. To quote Secretary of the Treasury Jack Lew: "The question to us is does that bill's restructuring authority work? It has to work or it's not going to be acceptable."

This will be one of the key questions we will look to our distinguished panel of witnesses to answer. While the bill contains a strong Oversight Board to ensure that Puerto Rico will make the tough decisions to get on a path of balanced budgets and sound fiscal practices, there are a number of other concerns we have about the bill and the process:

- We continue to insist that the Oversight Board should not impose further austerity, which will be counterproductive toward efforts to restore the island's economy.

- We question the merit of authorizing the transfer of thousands of acres of the Vieques National Wildlife Refuge away from the American people.

- We also stress, as the Treasury Department does, that Puerto Rico will be unable to make any fiscal plan work going forward, without the Medicaid support that is called for in the Treasury proposal and that such assistance be provided to the smaller territories as well.

- That Puerto Rico's underfunded pensions should not be raided to pay debt and that pensioners must be made whole.

- We cannot see the logic behind lowering the minimum wage to $4.25 an hour for the very group of people we need to stay on the island to anchor the recovery.

Mr. Chairman, you and your staff deserve to be commended for your willingness to work in an honest and forthright way to address the crisis in Puerto Rico. To that end I remain hopeful that we will be able to pass a bill out of the committee tomorrow that will enjoy the support of all Members and I continue to pledge to work with you to realize this goal. The people of Puerto Rico deserve no less.

————

The CHAIRMAN. Thank you.

The Vice Chair is not here and I would like to get to the panel as quickly as possible, but would be remiss if we do not get to the designee of the Ranking Minority Member, Mr. Pierluisi, since he has a little bit to do with this particular topic.

Mr. Pierluisi, you are recognized for an opening statement.

STATEMENT OF THE HON. PEDRO R. PIERLUISI, A REPRESENTATIVE IN CONGRESS FROM THE TERRITORY OF PUERTO RICO

Mr. PIERLUISI. Thank you.

Chairman Bishop, I want to begin by thanking you and your staff for the hard work you have put into this bill. You have been a gentleman, tough when you need to be, but always open and fair.

The CHAIRMAN. Wait, would you say that one more time? I will give you an extra 15 seconds. Especially after last night, would you say that just one more time?

Mr. PIERLUISI. You have been a gentleman, tough when you need to be, but always open and fair.

I know the responsibility you have been handed is heavy and at times thankless, but you and I, and our colleagues, should not lose sight of the stakes here and never forget how much what we are doing matters to regular people, whether it is a teacher in Aguadilla, a doctor in Ponce, a policeman in Mayaguez, a special-needs student in Caguas, or a middle-class family in San Juan or Salt Lake City who bought a Puerto Rico government bond and are concerned about their investment. If we cannot get a balanced, bipartisan bill to the President's desk, the consequences for Puerto Rico and the island's creditors are likely to be grave.

Trust me, there are provisions in this bill that I dislike, and there are items not in the bill, like equity under Medicaid and refundable tax credits, that I believe should have been included. It is easy to object to a bad provision in a bill or to the exclusion of a good provision from a bill and therefore to say "no" to a bill. But I respect those on both sides of the aisle who are looking at the bill holistically and working hard to get to a "yes."

The broad question I will pose to our witnesses today is this: Does the bill achieve its intended purpose, which is to help Puerto Rico address its current crisis and create the foundation for a brighter future?

Let me break the bill down into its component parts.

First, Title I and Title II establish a seven-member, temporary, independent oversight board, subject to strong ethics and conflict-of-interest rules, given specific responsibilities, that will terminate once certain conditions are satisfied.

Chairman Bishop and I worked together on those titles, and while this point is subject to reasonable debate, I believe these titles are a dramatic improvement over the earlier version of the bill and now, more or less, strike the appropriate balance between effectiveness in instilling fiscal discipline and respect for the democratic process.

The board's main function is to provide broad oversight over fiscal policymaking in Puerto Rico. The board will provide guardrails for the government of Puerto Rico, but in no way supplant the territory's elected leaders. The Governor will be responsible for developing a long-term fiscal plan, and the Governor and Legislative Assembly will be responsible for crafting annual budgets in line with that fiscal plan, subject to the board's ultimate approval.

During the fiscal year, compliance with the budget will be monitored, and any material variances between what was projected to occur and what is actually occurring will be identified. And Puerto Rico's elected leaders will have multiple opportunities to take remedial action as they deem appropriate. In short, the board will have a supervisory role and will only assume a more active, hands-on role as a last resort.

I will ask the witnesses whether they believe the board's powers are properly calibrated.

Second, section 206, Title III and Title IV, taken together, provide Puerto Rico with a debt-restructuring mechanism. Section 407 provides a territory government with a temporary stay of litigation, which, let me underscore, is intended to create an environment for consensual negotiations with creditors, not to encourage otherwise avoidable defaults.

Under the collective-action provision in Title VI, the oversight board will help debt-issuing entities in Puerto Rico and their creditors to try to reach voluntary agreements to restructure debt. If any entity reaches an agreement with a sufficient number of creditors, who will be grouped into pools or classes, that agreement will become binding on all the creditors in that pool. However, if an agreement cannot be reached, the board may authorize the entity to go to court and adjust that using the Bankruptcy Code provisions that apply in every state in the Nation.

So you see, the board is overseeing the debt-restructuring mechanism. I will ask the witnesses, especially Mr. Weiss, about these provisions of the bill, whether they are workable, and, if not, what changes need to be made to make them work.

Let me just give you the bottom line. This is the bottom line: My constituents and I will accept this oversight, provided—let me say again—provided we also get a meaningful debt-restructuring mechanism. Unless I get the witnesses and experts on this, starting with Treasury, to vouch that the debt-restructuring mechanism in this bill is acceptable and is going to provide the necessary relief to the government of Puerto Rico, I will not go for this bill.

And let me emphasize, we need to work, both sides of the aisle here. Otherwise, this is not going to happen. Puerto Rico is going to continue deteriorating, people are going to continue migrating to the states, and it is going to be an embarrassment not only for Puerto Rico, but for the United States at large.

That is the bottom line. Let's work. Let's work this bill. Let's get it done.

The CHAIRMAN. Thank you.

Mr. PIERLUISI. Thank you.

[The prepared statement of Mr. Pierluisi follows:]

PREPARED STATEMENT OF THE HON. PEDRO R. PIERLUISI, A REPRESENTATIVE IN CONGRESS FROM THE TERRITORY OF PUERTO RICO

Chairman Bishop, I want to begin by thanking you and your staff for the hard work you have put into this bill. You have been a gentleman—tough when you need to be, but always open and fair. I know the responsibility you have been handed is heavy and, at times, thankless. But you, and I, and our colleagues should not lose sight of the stakes here, and never forget how much what we are doing matters to regular people, whether it is a teacher in Aguadilla, a doctor in Ponce, a policeman in Mayaguez, a special needs student in Caguas, or a middle-class family in San Juan or Salt Lake City who bought a Puerto Rico government bond and is concerned about their investment. If we cannot get a balanced, bipartisan bill to the President's desk, the consequences for Puerto Rico and the island's creditors are likely to be grave. Trust me, there are provisions in this bill that I dislike, and there are items not in the bill—like equity under Medicaid and refundable tax credits—that I believe should have been included. It is easy to object to a bad provision in the bill, or to the exclusion of a good provision from the bill, and therefore to say "no" to the entire bill. But I respect those on both sides of the aisle who are looking at the bill holistically and working hard to get to "yes."

The broad question I will pose to our witnesses today is this: Does the bill achieve its intended purpose, which is to help Puerto Rico address its current crisis, and create the foundation for a brighter future?

Let me break the bill down into its component parts.

First, Title I and Title II establish a seven-member, temporary, independent oversight board, subject to strong ethics and conflict-of-interest rules, given specific responsibilities, that will terminate once certain conditions are satisfied. Chairman Bishop and I worked together on these titles, and—while this point is subject to reasonable debate—I believe these titles are a dramatic improvement over the earlier version of the bill and now more or less strike the appropriate balance between effectiveness in instilling fiscal discipline and respect for the democratic process. The board's main function is to provide broad oversight of fiscal policymaking in Puerto Rico. The board will provide guardrails for the government of Puerto Rico, but in no way supplant the territory's elected leaders. The Governor will be responsible for developing a long-term fiscal plan, and the Governor and legislative assembly will be responsible for crafting annual budgets in line with that fiscal plan, subject to the board's ultimate approval. During the fiscal year, compliance with the budget will be monitored, any material variances between what was projected to occur and what is actually occurring will be identified, and Puerto Rico's elected leaders will have multiple opportunities to take remedial action as they deem appropriate. In short, the board will have a supervisory role and will only assume a more active, hands-on role as a last resort. I will ask the witnesses whether they believe the board's powers are properly calibrated.

Second, Section 206, Title III, and Title VI, taken together, provide Puerto Rico with a debt restructuring mechanism. Section 407 provides the territory government with a temporary stay of litigation, which—let me underscore—is intended to create an environment for consensual negotiations with creditors and not to encourage otherwise avoidable defaults. Under the collective action provision in Title VI, the oversight board will help debt-issuing entities in Puerto Rico and their creditors try to reach voluntary agreements to restructure debt. If an entity reaches an agreement with a sufficient number of creditors, who will be grouped into pools or classes, that agreement will become binding on all creditors in that pool. However, if an agreement cannot be reached, the board may authorize the entity to go to court and adjust debt using the bankruptcy code provisions that apply in every state in the Nation. I will ask the witnesses, especially Mr. Weiss, about these provisions of the bill, whether they are workable, and—if not—what changes need to be made to make them work.

Thank you.

———

The CHAIRMAN. Let me now introduce our witnesses.

I appreciate all of you coming, many of you for a second time, to be with us here.

First, Mr. Antonio Weiss, who is the Counselor to the Secretary of the U.S. Department of the Treasury.

Thank you. Sorry you had such a difficult time in traffic getting up here.

The Honorable Anthony Williams, Senior Advisor for Dentons U.S. LLP and former Mayor of Washington, DC, as well as somebody who has been involved in these types of boards in the past.

Mr. John Miller, CFA, who is the Managing Director and Co-Head of Fixed Income, Nuveen Asset Management, from Chicago.

Thanks for being here.

Professor Andrew Kent, Professor of Law at Fordham University in New York.

Mr. Susheel Kirpalani—did I come close? Susheel. No, I wasn't even close. He is a partner from Quinn Emanuel Urquahart & Sullivan—even the company has a long name—also from New York.

Thank you for being here. And I will try to get the name right as we go from here on in.

And also, Professor Simon Johnson, who is a Professor of Global Economics and Management at MIT Sloan School of Management in Cambridge.

I also would like to mention that we did invite Mr. Timothy Lee from the Center for Individual Freedom to testify. However, he was obviously busy and declined to actually come and talk to us directly.

Let me remind the witnesses of the rule here. Your entire testimony is part of the record. The oral part we have right now has to be limited to 5 minutes. I would just remind you, I think you have all been here before, but if not, the lights in front of you, green is we are on a roll. When you have a minute left, the yellow light will appear. And when it is red, I really want you to stop in mid-sentence so we can get everything through. We will try and keep that 5 minutes as sacrosanct.

With that, the Chair now recognizes Mr. Weiss for your testimony.

STATEMENT OF ANTONIO WEISS, COUNSELOR TO THE SECRETARY, U.S. DEPARTMENT OF THE TREASURY, WASHINGTON, DC

Mr. WEISS. Chairman Bishop, Ranking Member Grijalva, and members of the committee, thank you for inviting Treasury to testify today.

We are encouraged by the seriousness of purpose that the committee has brought to this task. Significant progress has been made in designing the elements of the bill. But more work is required, as I will describe, to ensure a responsible solution to the escalating crisis in Puerto Rico. We look forward to continue working with you and your staff to further refine the legislation immediately following today's hearing.

As this committee is well aware, Puerto Rico is already in distress. The Commonwealth has already defaulted on its debt. Litigation is mounting. Puerto Rico has no access to credit markets, even the costliest ones.

The effects of the crisis become more evident each passing day. Health, education, and public safety services have been curtailed because the government is out of cash and cannot pay its bills. Suppliers are owed more than $2 billion. Hospitals have closed floors and terminated employees. The largest hospital system in Puerto Rico just notified its staff that it must lay off nearly 500 workers, 10 percent of its workforce.

Last week, the Governor was forced to declare a state of emergency for the GDB, the Commonwealth's key fiscal agent and lender of last resort. That action restricts the ability of Puerto Rico's agencies, municipalities, and other public instrumentalities from withdrawing deposits at the bank, and it threatens to disrupt many programs and services throughout the island. A moratorium on all debts of the Commonwealth has been authorized by the local legislature and may be invoked for the GDB, which has a major payment coming due in just 2 weeks.

In October of last year, as this committee knows, the Administration introduced a comprehensive plan that included four key elements: broad restructuring authorities, independent oversight, adequate funding of healthcare services, and incentives to drive economic growth.

While the Administration believes all elements of its legislative proposal are essential to arrest the crisis in Puerto Rico and set the stage for economic renewal, the legislation under consideration today attempts to address the two most urgent requirements: debt restructuring and fiscal oversight.

I commend the committee for producing draft legislation that seeks to provide Puerto Rico with those essential tools and attempts to do so in a way that provides the ability to reach a sustainable solution for all of Puerto Rico's debts. However, despite the progress that has been made, there are still vital questions of workability in the draft bill that must be resolved.

First, we support tools that facilitate voluntary restructurings, but the bill's version of a collective action clause imposes, in our judgment, an unworkable, mandatory process that will only delay the ability to reach a comprehensive resolution. Under the proposed approach, all of Puerto Rico's numerous debtors would have to complete a complicated process before any single entity could begin to restructure.

Second, any stay on litigation must ensure that the Commonwealth has sufficient breathing space to allow for voluntary negotiations, which we strongly support. A stay must also allow for a transition without interruption from these voluntary negotiations into a period of restructuring if it is needed. As drafted, there is risk that a stay may terminate prior to the commencement of restructuring, resulting in a gap and a chaotic race to the courthouse.

Third, the process for entering restructuring should not require a supermajority of the board. A minority of the board should not have veto power at the critical juncture when all other options have been exhausted.

Finally, the legislation must more evenly balance competing policy priorities. Undermining the minimum wage and overtime rules in Puerto Rico, thereby increasing disparities in pay between Puerto Rico and the mainland, is not a recipe for economic growth. And the legislation must offer a responsible process to ensure the retirement security of the 330,000 citizens in Puerto Rico that will depend on their pension benefits.

In short, while the committee has made great progress, there is additional work to do. If Congress does not act, the situation can only grow worse. Action is required today to protect the safety and economic well-being of the 3.5 million American——

The CHAIRMAN. Mr. Weiss, you have 2 seconds to finish up here.

Mr. WEISS [continuing]. Citizens of Puerto Rico. And we look forward to continuing working with you after this hearing.

11

[The prepared statement of Mr. Weiss follows:]

PREPARED STATEMENT OF MR. ANTONIO WEISS, COUNSELOR TO THE SECRETARY,
U.S. DEPARTMENT OF THE TREASURY, WASHINGTON, DC

Chairman Bishop, Ranking Member Grijalva, and members of the committee, thank you for inviting Treasury to testify today. We are encouraged by the seriousness of purpose that the committee has brought to this task. Significant progress has been made in designing the elements of the bill. But more work is required to ensure a responsible solution to the escalating crisis in Puerto Rico.

We look forward to continue working with you and your staff to further refine the legislation immediately following today's hearing.

URGENT SITUATION IN PUERTO RICO

As this committee is well aware, Puerto Rico is already in distress. The Commonwealth has already defaulted on its debt. Litigation is mounting. Puerto Rico has no access to credit markets, even the costliest ones. Puerto Rico's debt trades at prices between 10 and 70 cents on the dollar.

The effects of the crisis become more evident by the day. Health, education, and public safety services have been curtailed because the government is out of cash and cannot pay its bills. Suppliers are owed more than $2 billion. Hospitals have closed floors and terminated employees. The largest private hospital system in Puerto Rico recently notified its staff that it must layoff nearly 500 workers, 10 percent of its workforce.

There are inadequate funds to respond to the spreading Zika virus. Fuel supplies for the government's ambulances, police cars, and fire trucks are dangerously close to being cut off.

Last week, the Governor was forced to declare a state of emergency for the Government Development Bank (GDB), the Commonwealth's key fiscal agent and lender of last resort. That action restricts the ability of Puerto Rico's agencies, municipalities, and other public instrumentalities from withdrawing deposits held at the Bank. It also threatens to disrupt many programs and services throughout the Island.

A moratorium on all debts of the Commonwealth has been authorized and may be invoked for the GDB, which has a major payment coming due in 2 weeks.

COMMENTS ON THE PROPOSED LEGISLATION

In October of last year, the Administration introduced a comprehensive plan that included four core elements: broad restructuring authorities, independent oversight, adequate funding of healthcare services, and incentives to drive economic growth.[1]

While the Administration believes all elements of its legislative proposal are essential to arrest the crisis in Puerto Rico and set the stage for economic renewal, the legislation under consideration today attempts to address the two most urgent requirements: debt restructuring and fiscal oversight.

I commend the committee for producing draft legislation that seeks to provide Puerto Rico with those essential tools and attempts to do so in a way that provides the ability to reach a sustainable solution across all of Puerto Rico's debts. However, despite the progress that has been made, there are still vital questions of workability in the draft bill that must be resolved.

First, we support tools that facilitate voluntary restructurings. But the bill's version of a collective action clause imposes an unworkable, mandatory process that will only delay the ability to reach a comprehensive resolution. Under the proposed approach, all of Puerto Rico's numerous debtors would have to complete a complicated process before any single entity could begin to restructure.

Second, any stay on litigation must ensure that the Commonwealth has sufficient breathing space to allow for voluntary negotiations. A stay must also allow for a transition without interruption from voluntary negotiations to a period of restructuring, if needed. As drafted, there is a risk the stay may terminate prior to the commencement of a restructuring, resulting in a chaotic race to the courthouse.

Third, the process for entering restructuring should not require a super-majority vote of the Board. A minority of the Board should not have veto power at the critical juncture when all other options have been exhausted.

---

[1] Addressing Puerto Rico's Economic and Fiscal Crisis and Creating a Path to Recovery: Roadmap for Congressional Action. Dated October 21, 2015. Available at: https://www.whitehouse.gov/sites/default/files/roadmap_for_congressional_action_puerto_rico_final.pdf.

Finally, the legislation must more evenly balance competing policy priorities. Undermining the minimum wage and overtime rules in Puerto Rico, thereby increasing the disparities in pay between Puerto Rico and the mainland, is not a recipe for economic growth. Rather, we believe a locally administered Earned Income Tax Credit is a more powerful and effective way to stimulate the economy and encourage work. The Administration also opposes efforts to undermine the protection of the Vieques National Wildlife Refuge and other wildlife refuges nationally from development and environmental destruction.

And, the legislation must offer a responsible process to ensure the retirement security of the 330,000 citizens in Puerto Rico that will depend on their pension benefits.

CONCLUSION

In short, while the committee has made progress, there is additional work to do. If Congress does not act, the situation will only get worse. Action is required now to protect the safety and economic well-being of the 3.5 million American citizens in Puerto Rico.

———

The CHAIRMAN. Good answer.

Mayor Williams, we will turn to you, please.

STATEMENT OF THE HON. ANTHONY A. WILLIAMS, SENIOR STRATEGIC ADVISOR, DENTONS, U.S. LLP, WASHINGTON, DC; FORMER MAYOR OF WASHINGTON, DC

Mr. WILLIAMS. Mr. Chairman, Ranking Member, members of the committee, I think you will be pleased to know that I am going to summarize my oral testimony and just make some key points: one point being I applaud the committee, its staff, and Treasury for working together on a consensus approach to a pressing problem, not just for Puerto Rico, but a national problem as well. I speak as an American citizen with some experience in these matters, having served as a CFO under the control board, so to speak, in Washington, DC, and then later as mayor.

And the observations I would make would be, number one, I think the bill does well in installing a competent group of non-interested, disinterested if you will, professionals who can serve on the oversight board. As well, I would also observe and applaud the fact that the board will be equipped with the resources of skilled professional staff in order to perform its oversight duties.

I would further observe that an important part of the board's work would be working with officials in Puerto Rico on the establishment of a long-term budget and financial plan—and I think this is crucially important—and using that budget and financial plan as a basis, that financial information and settled expectations as a basis, for any debt restructuring or concessions that have to be made, recognizing—and I applaud this element of the bill—that the oversight board will ultimately serve as a facilitator and a convener to allow elected officials to take the first opportunity to seize advantage and see opportunity in this crisis.

An example of one area where I hope the board will use its influence with elected officials going forward is using its influence with elected officials to establish in Puerto Rico a strong financial entity—you could call it a financial director, you could call it a CFO—but, I would argue, to consolidate the treasury functions, the controllership functions, the budget functions in one person who has some degree—even after the control period, some degree of autonomy so that you have an umpire in the situation to call balls and strikes, set a revenue estimate that everybody respects.

The final observation I would make is, once the work of this bill is in place, expectations settled, and good stewardship has been established on the island, I would agree with the observation of Mr. Weiss that it is crucially important that economic incentives be in place to allow the economic renewal in Puerto Rico to go forward.

Those are my observations in summary, Mr. Chairman, and I look forward to answering your questions.

[The prepared statement of Mr. Williams follows:]

PREPARED STATEMENT OF ANTHONY A. WILLIAMS, SENIOR STRATEGIC ADVISOR TO DENTONS, U.S. LLP; FORMER MAYOR OF WASHINGTON, DC

On January 26, I submitted testimony to this committee in support of a bill the purpose of which was to provide Federal support to constructively address Puerto Rico's fiscal challenges and assist in its economic recovery. At the time, there was no bill, and, as such, my comments, drawn from my experience in working in concert with the control board that Congress created for Washington, DC, and later as its Mayor, were necessarily to provide a set of general considerations that this committee ought to consider in fashioning legislation. Now, only 2 months later, with much thanks for the earnest efforts of this committee and its seasoned and highly skilled professional staff, with the benefit of important insights and perspectives offered by the leadership at Treasury, there is such a bill and I wish to supplement my prior testimony to comment on it.

I am most pleased about the contents of the draft legislation and I come before this committee to endorse both its balance and the bipartisan efforts that necessarily were at the cornerstone of crafting it. Like most bills that gain support from competing perspectives, this bill, which offers a realistic set of provisions than can lead to a sustainable solution and a vibrant and financially healthy Puerto Rico, has aspects that each constituency likes and others that are less desired by the same constituency. Other constituencies have yet different likes about the bill and aspects they wish could be otherwise. But such is the nature of compromise, just as fostering compromise and consensual agreement are also to be at the heart of the contemplated oversight board's role if the legislation is enacted.

So why do I endorse the proposed bill and urge its adoption? At the outset, permit me to observe that many of the concepts that I felt would be fundamental to fiscal recovery legislation for Puerto Rico when I last spoke to this committee are in fact present in the proposed bill. Because many of the principles that made DC's board successful are also key elements of the Puerto Rican oversight legislation, I wish to highlight them as well as a couple of additional components that are especially well suited to address Puerto Rico's fiscal challenges.

First, the criteria established for selecting the oversight board's composition will assure input from seven well experienced professional members who will understand the complexities of government budgeting and operations and relevant legal and financial considerations that arise in fiscal distress situations. Importantly, too, some of its members are expected to either now live, grew up on the Island or have been involved in businesses there, and, as such, will have a deep appreciation for the culture and values of its people and institutions.

Second, the board is going to be fully staffed with an executive director and other important senior officials; and that's critical. There is much to be done; and to do its work, the board needs to develop a comprehensive understanding of the structures, workings and financial processes of the executive and legislative branches of Puerto Rico's government. Assembling a meaningful complement of sophisticated board employees, some importantly drawn from the Island's populace, is needed. Then, too, the board needs a talented team of legal and financial professionals to interface with similar professional who have been representing the Puerto Rican government and its creditors; and the legislation anticipates such retentions as well. As for the board's offices, the legislation contemplates that the board will be well staffed both in DC and in San Juan, and that, too, is vital to the board's success.

Third, Title II of the draft legislation gives the board a robust set of tools to work with Puerto Rican officials to develop viable cost saving solutions; and, clearly, the intent of the legislation is to have the board forge cooperation and reach a consensus among the government entities and their creditors to implement a series of well-conceived initiatives that are both tangible and attainable from the Common-

14

wealth's perspective, yet also factor in and respect the perspective of the Commonwealth's creditors. Unquestionably, there will need to be some belt-tightening if the
board is to effectively fulfill its mandate; and the legislation confers on the board
the means to fashion real solutions that will narrow the budgetary gaps being experienced by many of Puerto Rico's territorial-level government components—and, to
the fullest extent possible, accomplish its cost containment goals through hands-on
consensus building.

This leads to a fourth virtue of the legislation, namely, that before there were to
be any allocation of creditor concessions that might be needed to achieve the legislatively required balanced budgets, whether any such concessions would need to come
from labor interests or from bondholders, all reasonable means should first be em-
ployed to narrow the extent of budget deficits. As such, the centerpiece of the
board's work will be to look for ways to makes budget narrowing initiatives as palat-
able and constructive as possible, recognizing that accomplishing what the government can itself achieve through fiscal discipline is its fundamental obligation before
being entitled to ask others to contribute to a solution.

Fifth, and related, Title III of the bill vests the board with the ability to exercise
debt adjustment powers, something that I stated in my prior testimony is a vitally
necessary if the oversight board is to be effective. But, importantly, the legislation
clearly directs the board to invoke its debt adjustment powers only as a last resort.
What the bill, instead, unmistakably favors is that the board act as a facilitator and
honest broker in assisting creditors and the Commonwealth's various governments
in reaching an equitable resolution to allocate any shortfall that cannot be solved
through operational efficiencies and other cost saving. While having such debt adjustment powers is vital to the board's ability to effectively encourage the parties
to reach consensual accords, a resolution borne out of compromise is always preferable. Settlement of the challenging and complex issues that will arise is certainly
favored by the bill's requirement that all consensual solutions be exhausted before
any resort to the board's debt adjustment authority can be invoked. Implicit in that
directive is the recognition that reaching an agreed set of solutions not only expe-
dites the resolution process, it reduces both the cost and delays of an adversarial
process, and brings with it finality and certainty. The experience of contested pro-
ceedings in similar types of matters teaches that each of the benefits that can be
achieved through a consensual and non-judicial resolution process are real and
meaningful, and far preferable to a litigated battle over competing perspectives
about what is fair.

With those observations about what commends adoption of this committee's well-
conceived legislative proposal, afford me to conclude with two other observations:

While not in the present bill, I'd like to see Congress also consider legislation that
can provide economic incentives for new and meaningful investment in the Island's
economy. Too many talented people of Puerto Rico have found it necessary to leave
their homeland in search of jobs in the states; and affording a constructive and financially feasible opportunity for those who would like to return is both the right
thing to do and could bring with it real excitement for businesses and entrepreneurs
to invest in the Island's future. Puerto Rico has a rich and healthy past, and there
are compelling reasons for its economy to once again flourish. Legislation that can
help promote real economic growth opportunities on the Island ought to be something Congress ought soon adopt.

Let me close by addressing again the anxieties that naturally arise when some
form of government oversight is part of a resolution process. Yes, every situation
is unique; and while Puerto Rico's situation is clearly not the same as Washington,
Detroit, New York, Cleveland or Harrisburg, all of which have been under some
form of an oversight regime, at the outset of every such oversight process, there has
always been strenuously voiced complaints about having an additional govern-
mentally-created body be given authority to assist local elected leaders in finding
and guiding needed solutions. But the lessons drawn from other notable places that
were subject to oversight does instruct that if done with due respect for those in
public office, and with keen awareness of both community leadership and an eye on
business interests, good and sustainable solutions can and have occurred. New York,
once in serious financial troubles in the late 70s, is as vibrant and financially robust
as any large city in the world; and first hand I can attest to the fiscal distress that
was the marque of this city and that led Congress to act only 20 years ago; but look
at us now.

So, too, I believe if the oversight board does its job well, rather than disaffecting
the populace simply because it has been called into action, it can instead help forge
hope, cooperation, belief in a strong future, and generate a real desire of the people
of Puerto Rico to get behind and be part of the Island's financial and economic

15

rebirth. Unquestionably, these goals clearly stand at the heart of the proposed legislation; and I do believe it will not be long before we will be looking back at today, appreciating both the bipartisan leadership of Congress as well as the understanding of the Commonwealth Government and its creditors, who with their hard work and in the spirit of compromise have collectively brought us the legislation now proposed—legislation poised to help foster an exciting and sustainable future that Puerto Rico justly deserves while fairly treating its creditors.

———

The CHAIRMAN. Thank you.
Mr. Miller.

STATEMENT OF JOHN V. MILLER, CFA, MANAGING DIRECTOR, CO-HEAD OF FIXED INCOME, NUVEEN ASSET MANAGEMENT, CHICAGO, ILLINOIS

Mr. MILLER. Thank you, Chairman Bishop and Ranking Member Grijalva, for the committee's leadership on Puerto Rico and for the opportunity to speak with you today regarding the draft legislation to address the fiscal crisis in Puerto Rico. My name is John Miller, and I am Managing Director and Co-Head of Fixed Income at Nuveen Asset Management. I have spent my entire 23-year career researching and managing municipal bonds on behalf of investors, the last 20 years with Nuveen.

The team that I oversee currently manages over $113 billion in municipal securities, and within that team I am directly managing approximately $20 billion in the most credit-sensitive, high-yield municipal securities. In these roles, I am making investment decisions and transacting in the municipal market every day. And because I do so on behalf of Nuveen's clients, I am also speaking with financial advisers to individual investors nearly every day.

I highlight this in order to emphasize that I am in continuous contact with the concerns of long-term, dedicated municipal bond investors and I have a deep understanding of what drives increases and decreases in demand for municipal bonds over time and through historically significant municipal credit events such as this, as well as how investors evaluate a diverse array of credit risks in the marketplace.

So I am not here in an attempt to promote or degrade any specific Puerto Rican security. Nuveen has invested in a few Puerto Rican bonds in a few of our products, but our overall exposure is relatively small. However, I do care deeply about what happens next in Puerto Rico, what potential outcomes could mean for the broader municipal bond market, what could constitute positive or negative precedent, and what could constitute market contagion risk.

It is important to acknowledge that the financial distress already exists in Puerto Rico as well as the numerous complex, competing stakeholder claims, the nonpayment of which are very likely to trigger a massive amount of litigation in the relatively near future. Given the worsening conditions, Nuveen Asset Management believes that this draft legislation has the potential to create a framework under which orderly, fair, and transparent resolution can be achieved for bondholders while also fostering the conditions necessary for economic growth in Puerto Rico.

It is clear that the marketplace for Puerto Rican bonds is already anticipating restructuring. The highest valued security, which is the general obligation debt, is priced in trading generally between 58 cents on the dollar to 67 cents on the dollar. Yields for Puerto Rico debt average above 12 percent, while the yields of AAA municipal securities average just 2.6 percent. So, current pricing and current yields demonstrate that the market is already recognizing that default and debt restructuring are inevitable.

Even while Puerto Rican securities have fallen into this distressed territory, the broader municipal bond market has experienced consistent and steady appreciation since the end of the year 2013. And this appreciation has been coincident with individual investor demand growing, as measured by strong municipal bond mutual fund inflows, during each of the last 10 calendar quarters.

Much of the investor base in Puerto Rican securities has shifted from traditional mutual funds to nontraditional or opportunistic hedge funds. According to Morningstar, 75 percent of municipal bond mutual funds owned Puerto Rican securities in 2013, but that figure had dropped to less than 50 percent by the end of the year 2015. So this shift in holdings to hedge funds from mutual funds I think mitigates the risk to individual investors that are long-term dedicated to the muni market.

In addition to the shifts in investor allocations which have already occurred in anticipation of Puerto Rican restructuring, the draft legislation serves to substantially mitigate, if not eliminate, the concerns around negative legal precedent from municipal securities.

And I would highlight the critical difference between a U.S. territory, which is ultimately subject to the control of the U.S. Congress, versus a state, which has sovereignty in its fiscal matters. If the proposed legislation were to become law, this would be a territory-specific law and therefore not applicable to 98 percent of the municipal bonds in the marketplace, as they are issued by entities that are on the mainland.

It is our opinion that there is no legal budgetary or market-based reason to believe that a territorial-specific law would set a precedent for even the most fiscally stressed states. Even lower-rated states, such as Illinois, do not need and would not benefit from restructuring of their bonded debt. Admittedly, Illinois is currently mired in political gridlock and that clouds our near-term outlook, but we feel the state has the economic base and fiscal capacity to independently address its own budget and pension challenges.

Since the draft legislation began to circulate roughly 2 weeks ago, the municipal bond market has generally been steady and has continued to strengthen, with continued inflows into municipal bond mutual funds around the industry. In addition, Puerto Rican bond valuations specifically did not move down in reaction to the draft or the release of the draft. And, in contrast, it was the imposition of the Commonwealth debt moratorium which did serve to weaken Puerto Rican-specific securities in the marketplace, but not the possibility of U.S. congressional involvement.

The horizon to measure market reaction has been short-lived, but we believe that the territorial-specific nature of the legislation, the strength of an independent control board, the transparency, and fairness of a more orderly process, would all be features that are welcomed by the municipal bond market.

Thank you very much.

[The prepared statement of Mr. Miller follows:]

PREPARED STATEMENT OF JOHN MILLER, MANAGING DIRECTOR, CO-HEAD OF FIXED INCOME, NUVEEN ASSET MANAGEMENT, CHICAGO, ILLINOIS

Thank you, Chairman Bishop and Ranking Member Grijalva, for the committee's leadership on Puerto Rico and for the opportunity to speak with you today regarding the Draft Legislation to address Puerto Rico's fiscal crisis. My name is John Miller. I'm Managing Director and Co-Head of Fixed Income at Nuveen Asset Management. I have spent my entire 23-year career researching and managing municipal bonds on behalf of investors, the last 20 with Nuveen. The team that I oversee currently manages over $113 billion of tax-exempt municipals. Within that team, I directly manage approximately $20 billion of the most credit sensitive, high-yield municipal securities. In these roles, I am making investments and transacting in the municipal market every day, and because I do so on behalf of Nuveen's clients, I am also speaking with Financial Advisors to individual investors nearly every day. I highlight this in order to emphasize that I am in continuous contact with the concerns of long-term dedicated municipal bond investors. I have a deep understanding of what drives increases and decreases in demand for municipal bonds over time and through historically significant municipal credit events such as this, as well as how investors evaluate a diverse array of credit risks in the marketplace.

I am not here in an attempt to promote or degrade any specific Puerto Rican security. While Nuveen is invested in a few Puerto Rican bonds in a few of our products, our overall exposure on behalf of clients is relatively small. However, I care deeply about what happens next in Puerto Rico, and what the potential outcomes could mean for the broader municipal bond market, what could constitute a positive or a negative precedent, and what could constitute market contagion risk.

It is important to acknowledge the financial distress that already exists in Puerto Rico, as well as the numerous and complex competing stakeholder claims, the non-payment of which are very likely to trigger a massive amount of prolonged litigation in the near future. Given these worsening conditions, we at Nuveen Asset Management believe the draft legislation has the potential to create a framework under which an orderly, fair and transparent resolution can be achieved for bondholders, while also fostering the conditions necessary for economic growth in Puerto Rico.

It is clear that the marketplace for Puerto Rican bonds is already anticipating a restructuring. The highest valued security, General Obligation or GO debt, is currently priced at between $58 and $64 per $100 of outstanding debt. Yields for Puerto Rico's debt average above 12 percent while the yields of AAA municipal securities average 2.6 percent. Current pricing and yields demonstrate the market already recognizes default and debt restructuring are inevitable.

Even while Puerto Rican securities have fallen into this distressed territory, the broader municipal bond market has experienced a consistent and steady appreciation since year-end 2013, and this appreciation has been coincident with steady increases in individual investor demand as measured by strong municipal bond mutual fund in-flows during each of the last 10 calendar quarters.

Much of the investor base of Puerto Rican securities has shifted from traditional mutual funds to non-traditional or opportunistic hedge funds. According to Morningstar, 75 percent of municipal bond mutual funds owned some Puerto Rican securities in 2013, versus less than 50 percent by the end of 2015. This shift in holdings to hedge funds from mutual funds mitigates the risks to retail investors.

In addition to the shifts in investor allocations which have already occurred in anticipation of a Puerto Rican restructuring, the draft legislation serves to substantially mitigate, if not eliminate, the concerns around negative legal precedent for municipal securities. I would highlight the critical difference between a U.S. Territory, which is ultimately subject to the control of the U.S. Congress, versus a state which has sovereignty in its fiscal matters. If the proposed legislation were to become Law, this would be a Territory specific law, and therefore not applicable to 98 percent of the municipal bonds in the marketplace as they are issued by entities that are on the mainland.

It is our opinion there is no legal, budgetary or market-based reason to believe that this Territorial-specific legislation would set a precedent for even the most fiscally stressed states. Even lower rated states, like Illinois, do not need and would not benefit from restructuring bonded debt. While admittedly Illinois is currently mired in political gridlock which clouds our near-term outlook, the state still has the economic base and fiscal capacity to independently address its budget and pension challenges.

Since the draft legislation began to circulate roughly 2 weeks ago, the municipal bond market has generally been steady and has actually strengthened, with continued inflows into municipal bond funds across the industry. In addition, Puerto Rican bonds valuations specifically did not move down in reaction to the release of the Draft. In contrast, it was actually the Commonwealth's debt moratorium legislation which served to weaken the marketplace for Puerto Rican securities recently, not the possibility of U.S. congressional involvement. While the time horizon to measure market reaction has been short lived, we believe the Territorial-specific nature of the legislation, the strength of an independent control board, the transparency and fairness that a more orderly process could bring, would all be features welcomed by the municipal bond market.

Thank you for the opportunity to testify today and I welcome your questions.

*****

White Paper Submitted for the Record by Mr. Miller

Puerto Rico's Course Forward

NUVEEN Asset Management

MARKET COMMENTARY
FEBRUARY 2016

By: Molly Shellhorn, Vice President, Senior Research Analyst and Shawn P. O'Leary, Senior Vice President, Senior Research Analyst

The next few months will be critical to determining Puerto Rico's future. With large debt service payments looming in May and July, and Congressional action becoming increasingly likely, events are quickly moving the Commonwealth to a point where the government's stance toward creditors could become more adversarial in the near term. In this paper we briefly review Puerto Rico's current fiscal situation, the Commonwealth's proposals thus far, and what we expect from the federal government.

We also explore how the Commonwealth's competing priorities are likely to stack up against one another given limited resources to pay all obligations in full. General obligation and COFINA (Puerto Rico Sales Tax Financing Corporation) bondholders may soon be engaged in a bitter inter-creditor battle while simultaneously competing with more sympathetic pensioners.

We then consider whether debt restructuring in Puerto Rico actually threatens the stability of the municipal market. Puerto Rico's unique situation will not likely set a broad precedent for either the market or other municipal issuers, but opponents of restructuring have claimed otherwise. We'll demonstrate that Puerto Rico truly is an outlier, and why we think its fiscal distress should stay contained to the island. Regardless of what transpires going forward, untangling Puerto Rico's difficulties will be a lengthy process. Investors should not expect a quick resolution.

Puerto Rico's Economic Situation Is Critical

Puerto Rico's economic challenges persist, and the catalyst for a turnaround is unclear. The Commonwealth has been in recession since 2006 primarily due to the expiration of federal tax incentives that previously incentivized U.S. firms to operate on island. Between 2009 and 2014, Puerto Rico's real national product declined 2.3%. Puerto Rico's planning board estimates another decline of 0.7% for the current fiscal year.

Unemployment remains very high at 12.2% as of December 2015, and labor force participation remains well below average at 45.5%. Median family income in Puerto Rico is just 34.4% of the U.S., and the poverty rate is an elevated 46.2%. Total nonfarm employment has stabilized, down only 0.3% year-over-year in December 2015, but employment is still 15% below peak levels reached in 2005.

Economic contraction and a lack of job opportunities have encouraged significant out-migration, particularly among working-age residents and young families. Between 2010 and 2015, Puerto Rico's population dropped an estimated 6.7%. Out-migration threatens to permanently erode Puerto Rico's economic base and ultimately the government's ability to structurally balance the budget.

As tax revenues suffered over the last decade, the government relied on tax increases and long-term borrowing to cover annual operating deficits rather than cut expenditures or address inefficiencies, poor tax compliance and corruption. A long history of overestimating revenues and lack of budgetary control only exacerbated the structural budget gap and overreliance on debt to fund operating expenses.

Following significant rating downgrades into junk territory and growing market concern about debt affordability, Puerto Rico has essentially lost market access to continue borrowing for cash flow. The government recently lowered general fund revenue expectations to $9.21 billion from $9.46 billion for the current fiscal year, and projects the government is at "risk of not having sufficient liquid resources to meet obligations as they come due."

Specifically, the government warned that Puerto Rico may be unable to make the Government Development Bank's (GDB) $422 million debt service payment due May 1, followed by a significant $1.3 billion payment due July 1 for general obligation (GO) and Commonwealth-guaranteed debt.

Restructuring Efforts Fall Short

It is against this context Puerto Rico is struggling to find a sustainable path forward. Months after Governor Alejandro García Padilla declared the Commonwealth's debt unpayable (signaling the potential for future debt impairment), creditors have generally dismissed the government's attempts to demonstrate the severity of Puerto Rico's fiscal gap. Last fall, the governor's working group released a *Fiscal and Economic Growth Plan* (FEGP), providing a multiyear projection of revenues and expenses that identified a cumulative $14 billion financing gap over the next five years. In January, the 5-year gap was revised up to $16.1 billion, and the 10-year financing gap was pegged at nearly $24 billion.

Sizeable multiyear deficit projections underlie the Commonwealth's recent offer to creditors to exchange existing bonds for new securities. The exchange, which we view as highly unlikely to be accepted by creditors outside of a formal restructuring process that includes a means of binding holdout creditors, would provide holders of $49.2 billion of various classifications of Puerto Rico debt with two new securities: $26.5 billion of base bonds and $22.7 billion of growth bonds. The plan cuts the debt by approximately 46% and includes a moratorium on all debt service through 2018, and then only interest payments until 2021.

The exchange offer proposes that holders of GO, sales tax-backed and other securities would exchange their bonds for differing amounts of base bonds, thus yielding varying levels of haircuts for different classifications of bondholders. The base bonds would be guaranteed by a new securitization of various government revenues and provide Puerto Rico with a lower, more level debt service structure. The growth bonds would only be paid if Puerto Rico's economic activity and resultant revenue collection meets or exceeds certain benchmarks.

In our view, there is little chance bondholders will readily exchange their securities in numbers sufficient to generate the savings contemplated by the Commonwealth. We believe the exchange offer is actually the Commonwealth's attempt to demonstrate to Congress the futility of reaching an orderly adjustment of debts outside the confines of a formal debt restructuring process supervised by a control board and/or federal courts.

Congress May Be Ready to Act

Until recently, it was unclear if Puerto Rico would generate enough momentum to motivate Congress to address the island's distress. U.S. lawmakers, now educated on Puerto Rico's precarious situation, may finally be ready to act. House Speaker Paul Ryan promised that Congress would address Puerto Rico's crisis by March 31, and his intent to get new legislation passed appears to be serious.

Initially, the division between Republicans and Democrats was clear. Republicans rejected anything considered a bailout for Puerto Rico and advocated further austerity measures. In contrast, Senate Democrats sent a letter to House leadership at the end ofJanuary urging quick passage of legislation granting the Commonwealth access to Chapter 9 bankruptcy. The letter said any bill that does not include bankruptcy would not be a "real solution" for Puerto Rico. U.S. Treasury Secretary Jack Lew has been clear about the current administration's support for both funding equity for federal programs and access to a broad debt restructuring regime.

Several Republican bills were proposed at the end of 2015. One granted the Commonwealth access to Chapter 9 if Puerto Rico agreed to a strong fiscal control board. Another called for a control board and provided additional aid. Given recent Congressional hearings and statements from ranking members, we expect additional legislative proposals to emerge soon. Senate Finance Committee Chair Orrin Hatch announced his intention to bring another bill in the near term and meet Speaker

Ryan's March 31 deadline for Congressional action. Additional hearings are scheduled in February.

We expect legislation providing a fiscal control or fiscal stabilization board with broad authority to be introduced and considered in the near term. Puerto Rico's long record of poor fiscal management, overlaid on a sprawling web of interconnected events and overly complex debt structure, demonstrates the need for federal intervention.

We now believe Congressional action appears both likely and necessary. A strong federal control board now seems to be inevitable and the opposition on the island has softened. External control and enforcement is likely the only way Puerto Rico can achieve structural reforms, implement difficult but necessary budgetary realignment, establish the conditions for economic growth and reestablish credibility with investors and thus access to the traditional municipal market.

The debate is not about whether a control board is necessary, but about how much authority the board should be given. The structure and authority of the new oversight entity must be carefully crafted to respect Puerto Rico's right to self-governance and hopefully be oriented toward establishing a foundation for future economic growth. Governmental reforms, improving fiscal policies, tax compliance and financial reporting are all critical to restoring credit quality and market credibility.

It remains unclear if legislation establishing a control board will be paired with a legal framework to adjust Puerto Rico's long-term debt and pension liabilities. The Commonwealth has attempted a consensual debt restructuring, but we are not surprised that these efforts have not yet gained sufficient traction with creditors, especially in light of the initial proposal.

Given the wide variety and complexity of Puerto Rico's debt obligations, the diversity of bondholders and interests involved, and the competing security pledges, realists will acknowledge there is little to no hope of a consensual resolution. Without some mechanism to bind holdout creditors, either through some form of bankruptcy or a broader collective action clause that would allow a majority bondholder vote to impose terms on holdouts, Puerto Rico is destined for years of litigation.

Treasury officials estimate it could take a decade to untangle competing creditor claims if the situation devolves into a web of competing litigation. Years of litigation and inter-creditor disputes will only stifle economic growth and accelerate out-migration, further diminishing the tax base available to pay off creditors.

We believe the final legislation must include a path for Puerto Rico to restructure these liabilities. We don't advocate for restructuring authority lightly. As investors, we prefer political solutions that avert restructurings whenever possible. Yet we believe when an issuer reaches the point where debt reduction becomes inevitable, any delay only serves to engage in value destruction through additional unsustainable borrowings, economic contraction and/or population loss due to reduced government services.

Thus the restructuring—painful as it may be—provides greater value to creditors than lobbying for maintaining the status quo. Puerto Rico's recent trend of increasingly expensive and onerous debt to bridge one fiscal year to the next offered the Commonwealth little chance of addressing its core problems: economic contraction, a declining population, a bureaucratic and inefficient government and a back-ended debt structure requiring annual cycles of painful budgetary decisions coupled with new and/or higher taxes. As municipal asset managers and creditors, we are reluctant to support any adjustment of debts by issuers, but we believe it is both inevitable and necessary for Puerto Rico.

Priorities Compete: GO, COFINA and Pensions

The absolute size of Puerto Rico's true fiscal gap is still unknown. The impact of future expenditure cuts and potential economic growth will hopefully moderate the $16 billion five-year gap projected by the governor's working group. However, even if the gap is reduced, it's clear to most that Puerto Rico will struggle to fully fund all general obligation (GO) and guaranteed debt while leaving COFINA obligations and pensions unimpaired.

We see GO, COFINA and pensions as the three main expenditures in direct competition for the government's limited resources. It is difficult to envision a scenario that avoids an inter-creditor legal battle between GO and COFINA bondholders, and we see all creditors in direct competition with pension beneficiaries.

GO and COFINA bondholders' interests are in direct opposition. GO debt benefits from a constitutional first priority on Commonwealth resources, but the COFINA corporation was constructed with the intention of exempting sales tax revenues from the definition of available resources for GO debt.

If GO debt is ever impaired in a future default, potentially as soon as this year, Puerto Rico will face lawsuits from GO investors demanding the government reclassify sales/VAT taxes to be considered available revenues to be redirected to GO debt service first.

Similarly, should the government attempt to divert sales tax revenues away from COFINA to GO debt, COFINA bondholders will litigate to protect their revenue pledge. It does not escape notice that the current debt restructuring proposal contemplates replacing COFINA's arguably successful securitization structure with a new securitized debt structure—essentially threatening to blow up one securitization in favor of another.

GO and guaranteed debt and COFINA debt represent the two largest categories of tax-supported debt. Given that these two together represent over 60% of tax supported debt and as the government is saying it can only afford to fund a much smaller fraction of current debt service, it is unlikely both will emerge from this process unscathed. Some creditors and on-island politicians have argued passionately that the constitutional priority of GO debt must be upheld and the rule of law cannot be set aside. However, we believe many market commentators and some Puerto Rican elected officials too liberally interpret the Puerto Rico Constitution to mean that GO bonds and other forms of guaranteed public debt cannot be restructured. A plain reading of the constitution reveals there is no such protection from an adjustment of the terms of Puerto Rico's constitutionally guaranteed debt.

The Puerto Rican constitution clearly establishes that GO and guaranteed debt have first priority on available resources. Existing statutes further support the constitutional priority establishing priority norms for the disbursement of public funds. Payment of principal and interest on debt service is specified as the first priority, specifically senior to expenditures for health, safety, education, welfare and retirement systems, which all rank third on the priority list. This should not, in our opinion, be read to describe anything other than a year-to-year prioritization of debt service coming due for the purposes of constructing a budget.

We believe Puerto Rico could theoretically implement a restructuring process for GO and Commonwealth-guaranteed debt, reduce the principle amount outstanding through that process and assert that their constitutional burden is met by making the now-reduced public debt the first budgetary priority. In other words, the constitution says only that public debt has a first priority on resources—whether that debt represents legacy debt at 100-cents on the dollar or restructured debt at 50-cents on the dollar. It is silent as to the adjustment of public debt.

The constitutional first priority on available resources for the benefit of public debt does not, in our opinion, preclude the possibility of debt restructuring or impairment. Puerto Rico could attempt to restructure constitutionally guaranteed obligations and subsequently argue that the new debt will maintain a first payment priority, post-restructuring. Puerto Rico has warned for years of the potential need to reprioritize essential services ahead of other obligations, including the public debt. In practical terms, this means subverting the "priority norms" established by law to the extent resources are insufficient to meet both debt service and the cost of providing essential services.

Though some observers point to the constitution and priority norms as evidence GO debt cannot be impaired, this idea has been undermined repeatedly by the territory's own risk disclosure statements in investor communications. For example, in March 2014, officials disclosed that "to the extent Commonwealth resources are diverted to such essential services, there is no assurance that the Commonwealth will have sufficient revenues to pay debt service on GO debt."

More recently, in the unaudited draft *Fiscal 2014 Basic Financial Statements*, the government stated it may amend the Organic Act that establishes these priorities or enact new emergency legislation that could include a debt moratorium on the payment of debt service. In short, Puerto Rico has been signaling to investors for years its intention to reprioritize essential services over debt.

Whether pension payments will be prioritized over debt is not yet apparent. In the government's first debt restructuring proposal to creditors, both GO and COFINA bonds received significant haircuts while pensions were notably absent. Puerto Rico's pension obligations are virtually entirely unfunded and growing rapidly. As of June 30, 2014, the unfunded pension liability is estimated at $43.6 billion across three retirement systems. The Employees Retirement System has the largest liability, at $30.2 billion, and the lowest funded ratio at 0.42%. Pension costs will soon be funded on a pay-go basis, increasing budgetary pressure. By fiscal 2018, pay-go pension payments could reach $2 billion per year, or nearly 20% of general fund revenues.

Preserving pension security is one of the administration's stated objectives. We believe the government will attempt to keep pensions free from impairment and prioritize these payments above debt service, regardless of current statutes that prioritize debt service ahead of annual pension costs. Threats to enact new legislation reversing the priority of payments support this. Additionally, the administration's current debt restructuring proposal does not include any changes or reductions for pension beneficiaries. We believe Puerto Rico intends to leave pension benefits untouched while attempting to impose haircut on all other long-term liabilities, even those with a guarantee and a dedicated pledged revenue.

Contagion Risk Is Low

Municipal investors are asking if a Puerto Rico restructuring will negatively impact the broader market. Growing evidence suggests Puerto Rico is now effectively separated from the traditional high yield market, let alone the overall municipal market. We believe most institutional investors understand Puerto Rico's unique situation, and the coming debt restructuring will not create widespread negative credit implications for other issuers.

Municipal investors should note that recent debt adjustments in a handful of California cities, Detroit and other jurisdictions did not disrupt the market. Detroit filed for bankruptcy protection on July 18, 2013, and on that day the AAA Municipal Market Data (MMD) 30-year yield was 4.03%. By December 31, 2015, the AAA MMD yield rallied by 121 basis points to 2.82%. As of this writing on February 19, 2016, AAA MMD stands at 2.78%, 125 basis points tighter than the day Detroit filed for bankruptcy.

Simultaneously, Puerto Rico's stance toward financial market creditors became increasingly hostile, from proposals to restructure debt and the beginning of what we expect will be a string of ongoing defaults. Municipal investors, rightly, continue to differentiate between individual pockets of credit stress and the much healthier overall market. We see no reason this will change based on how Congress addresses Puerto Rico's situation.

Market differentiation between Puerto Rican bonds and other high yield municipal bonds started even before the rating agencies downgraded Puerto Rico debt to below investment grade in 2013. Since then, divergence between Puerto Rico and the rest of the high yield market can been seen in credit spreads, fund flows and total returns.

Exhibit 1 shows credit spreads for high yield indices with and without Puerto Rico. Since the beginning of 2014, high yield credit spreads excluding Puerto Rico securities narrowed 30 basis points, while spreads including Puerto Rico securities widened over 120 basis points. The market has clearly identified elevated risk for Puerto Rico debt, while spreads for other high yield municipals are more in line with historic norms.

Exhibit 1: Spreads Including Puerto Rico Have Widened

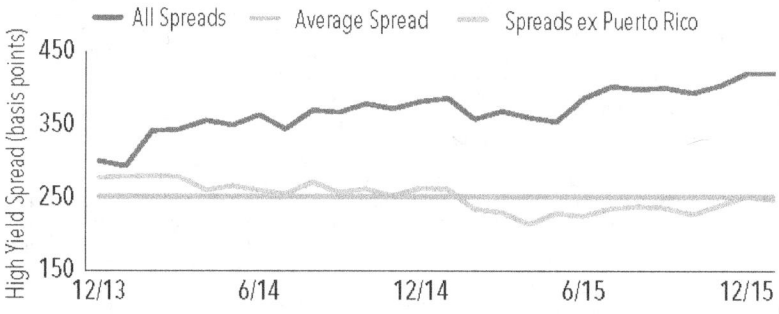

Source: Barclays Capital. Data from 12/31/13 to 1/31/16. Past performance is no guarantee of future results.

Investors have already differentiated between funds with and without Puerto Rico holdings. The difference in net flows for funds with elevated Puerto Rico exposure versus funds with minimal Puerto Rico exposure is notable. Since the beginning of 2014, funds with a less than 5% allocation of net assets to Puerto Rico reported inflows of $12.6 billion, equivalent to 40% of beginning assets under management (AUM), as shown in Exhibit 2. Over the same time period, high yield funds with more than 5% allocated to Puerto Rico have experienced outflows totaling 8.75% of AUM. This trend of diverging investor flows was sizable, orderly and largely unnoticed by market participants.

High yield municipal funds with less than 5% allocation to Puerto Rico now represent double the AUM of high yield municipal funds with more than 5% exposure to Puerto Rico. At the start of 2014 that figure was only 28% more in AUM.

Exhibit 2:
High Yield Funds Including Puerto Rico Experienced Outflows

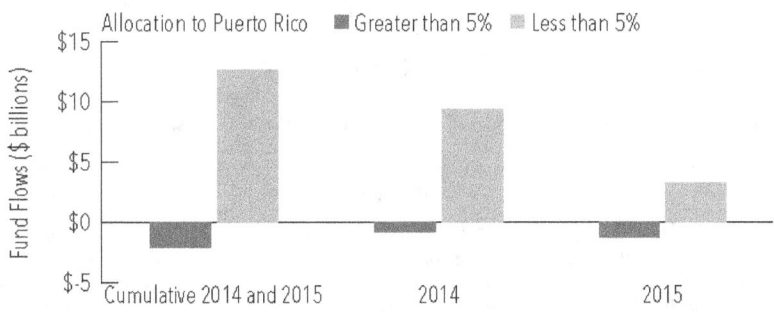

Source: Morningstar Direct.

High yield returns without Puerto Rico have also outperformed each year since 2013 and the difference has increased each year. Based on the S&P High Yield Municipal Index, high yield returns without Puerto Rico were 1.47% and 4.29% higher in 2014 and 2015, respectively, than the index when Puerto Rico is included.

A Threat to Tax-Exemption Is Possible

We don't see Puerto Rico creating contagion for the municipal market via investor reticence over purchasing securities from mainland states, other municipal issuers scrambling to seek debt relief or a general increase in municipal borrowing costs.

However, market contagion is possible in the form of threats to the municipal bond tax exemption. The longer Puerto Rico remains unaddressed by Congress and unable to appropriately restructure its debts and unfunded pension liabilities, the longer Puerto Rico will remain in the headlines. As this plays out, the potential only grows for some members of Congress to view Puerto Rico's profligate spending and use of debt to fund government services as representative of the entire municipal market.

Of course, any curtailment of the municipal tax exemption on the basis of Puerto Rico's debt abuse would be wholly unfair to the rest of the market. Puerto Rico spent much of the last 10 years issuing billions in debt to pay maturing debt and fund government services, while overall municipal debt outstanding remained more or less constant. Exhibit 3 shows the total municipal debt outstanding from 2005 through 2014.

24

Exhibit 3:
Total Municipal Debt Outstanding Has Remained Constant

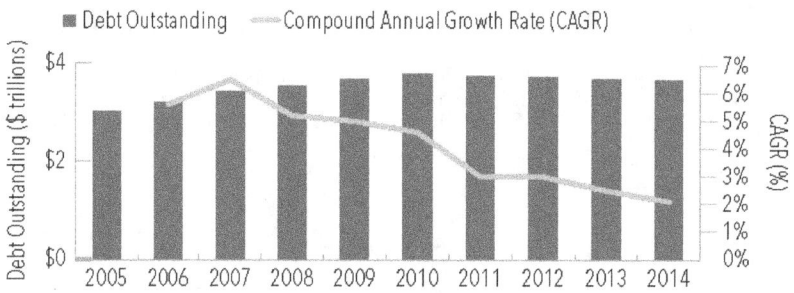

Source: Securities Industry and Financial Markets Association. Most recent data available.

From 2005 through 2010, municipal debt outstanding grew from $3 trillion to $3.77 trillion as the housing market boom created abundant property taxes, permit fees and other revenues related to robust residential growth. This growth also created the need for new schools, roads, bridges and expanded water and sewer treatment capacity. Since the onset of the recession, however, municipal debt outstanding actually declined to $3.65 trillion. Issuers slowed the pace of capital investment, and refunding transactions—rather than new money issuance for projects—represented the majority of municipal debt issuance. From 2005 through 2014, total municipal market debt outstanding grew at a 2.1% compound annual growth rate (CAGR). This period included several years of healthy capital investment to accommodate residential growth.

We think this manageable trend in municipal debt issuance speaks to municipal market issuers' long-standing history of using municipal bonds—and the benefit of municipal tax exemption—to responsibly invest in the country's critical infrastructure. Puerto Rico and a limited number of other municipal issuers that rely on municipal bonds to maintain government spending do not represent the broader market, nor do they indicate the general health of states and municipalities.

While Puerto Rico's approximately $70 billion of debt makes the Commonwealth one of the largest issuers of municipal bonds, it represents just 1.9% of municipal debt outstanding. Reducing or eliminating the municipal tax exemption based on the actions of Puerto Rico is like treating a sprained toe by removing the patient's leg.

Could Puerto Rico Set a Negative Precedent?

We do not believe a broad debt restructuring in Puerto Rico would lead states struggling with budgetary challenges (such as Illinois, New Jersey and Pennsylvania) to clamor to restructure their own debt. Puerto Rico attempting to restructure its obligations won't encourage other states to do the same. The magnitude of Puerto Rico's debt and the lack of an economic base to service long-term liabilities makes it a significant outlier in comparison to other states. The "Illinois is next" argument misleadingly suggests that Illinois—admittedly the least creditworthy U.S. state—is comparable to Puerto Rico in terms of financial stress and capacity to meet its obligations.

Comparing key credit metrics for Puerto Rico and Illinois, as shown in Exhibit 4, reveals this argument to be quite lacking.

Exhibit 4: Illinois Is Not Comparable to Puerto Rico

	Puerto Rico	Illinois
Economic and Demographic Data		
2015 Population (est)	3,474,182	12,859,995
GDP	$103.1 B	$745.9 B
Unemployment Rate (Dec 2015)	12.2%	5.9%
Labor Force Participation Rate	45.5%	65.9%
Number of Households	1.2 M	4.8 M
Median Household Income	$19,686	$57,166
Mean Household Income	$30,756	$76,521
Total Household Income	$38.2 B	$365.7 B
Poverty Rate	46.2%	14.4%
Taxation Rates		
Sales Tax	11.5%	6.25%
Individual Income Tax	7% - 33% (graduated)	3.75% (flat)
Liabilities		
Net Tax Supported Debt	$55.5 B	$34.5 B
Unfunded Pension Liabilities	$43.6 B	$111.0 B
Comparative Ratios		
Net Tax Supported Debt / Total Household Income	145.4%	9.4%
Net Tax Supported Debt & Unfunded Pension Liabilities / Total Household Income	259.6%	39.8%
Net Tax Supported Debt / Gross Domestic Product	53.8%	4.6%
Net Tax Supported Debt & Unfunded Pension Liabilities / Gross Domestic Product	96.1%	19.5%

Sources: BEA.gov, BLS.gov, U.S. Census, State of Illinois FY2014 CAFR, Commonwealth of Puerto Rico FY2013 CAFR, Commonwealth of Puerto Rico Financial Information and Operating Data Report, November 6, 2015, Moody's 2015 Debt Medians, Federal Reserve Bank of St. Louis.

Illinois is certainly not a model of state governance and fiscal responsibility. But the size of the state's economy and tax base, and its comparatively low sales and income tax rates, demonstrate the state has far more flexibility to address its long-term obligations than Puerto Rico. The state's diverse economy ranks fifth overall in the U.S. in terms of gross domestic product (GDP), and fourth in per capita income among the 10 most populous states. Though the state's recovery has lagged the U.S., it is still growing modestly, unlike Puerto Rico.

The scope of Puerto Rico's challenges far outstrips those of Illinois once debt and unfunded liabilities are indexed to the respective government's economies and resident incomes. Debt and unfunded pension liabilities represent just 19.5% and 39.8% of Illinois GDP and total household income, respectively. Puerto Rico carries debt and unfunded pension liabilities representing 96.1% and 259.6% of GDP and total household income, respectively. Simply put, Puerto Rico is much more leveraged than even Illinois, the lowest-rated U.S. state. It is inappropriate to compare them interchangeably in the context of the need for federally sanctioned debt relief.

A political impasse has left Illinois operating without an adopted budget almost nine months into the fiscal year. The budget standoff has resulted in a growing accounts payable balance and reduced liquidity, and distracted state leaders from addressing pension underfunding, which remains a serious threat to the state's long-term financial stability and structural budget balance. Failing to pass a budget and address pensions has undoubtedly weakened the state's ability to withstand the next economic downturn. Illinois deserves its lowest-rated state designation.

But Illinois' budget stalemate, while detrimental to the state's economy, is a political battle rather than a crisis caused by economic contraction or a fundamental inability to afford long-term obligations. The state's budget gap for fiscal 2017 is now projected to increase to $5.6 billion, or 17% of estimated revenues. While not insignificant, this budget gap is far from insurmountable. Increasing the individual income tax rate by 1.25% to 5.0% (from 3.75%) would generate more than $4.1 billion in new revenue, and go a long way to close the annual revenue gap. The mathematical gap in Illinois is not nearly as wide as the political chasm. While restructuring debt seems both appropriate and unavoidable for Puerto Rico, it is not the appropriate tool for Illinois and would provide the state with little budget relief.

Some argue that Puerto Rico's indebtedness is overstated in comparison to mainland U.S. states, as Puerto Ricans pay no federal income tax and therefore don't feel the burden of the U.S. government's debt. Once again, we believe this argument is designed to mislead rather than inform. It inappropriately equates two very different types of debt: municipal debt issued by state and local governments and sovereign debt of the United States.

Unlike state and local government debt, sovereign debt of the United States is not truly amortized with regular principal payments. Rather, sovereign debt is very often rolled into new debt offerings with only the interest cost borne in the budget. Sovereigns tend to attempt to maintain their debt outstanding within a specific range of economic output (such as GDP), allowing the nominal amount of debt to grow over time but remaining within a measure of affordability as determined by economic activity. Thus any attempt to lump total federal government debt outstanding into state debt profiles is an attempt to inflate state indebtedness to give Puerto Rico's debt the veneer of affordability.

A more appropriate way to consider the impact of the federal government's debt is to consider annual interest cost, which in fiscal year 2015 amounted to $402.4 billion. On a per capita basis, the annual interest cost on federal debt was $1,252 in fiscal year 2015—or just 4.2% of Illinois' per capita income. The federal government's debt is not an oppressive fiscal constraint on the U.S. states and taxpayers. Nor does it make Puerto Rico's debt load magically affordable.

It is similarly inappropriate to contend Puerto Rico's debt burden is artificially inflated in comparison to the states because it includes all debt issued for underlying municipalities and schools, whereas Illinois' total debt does not. This is also a spurious argument because debt issued and guaranteed by Puerto Rico's general government and the GDB is their responsibility and supported by their revenues. In contrast, all Illinois taxpayers are not responsible for debt issued by every underlying school district or county.

When the affordability of Puerto Rico's debt burden is debated, some claim that the Commonwealth doesn't fully capture all economic activity and their debt, and pensions would be affordable if only they boosted tax compliance. While we agree that Puerto Rico does a poor job of tax compliance and collection, we're not convinced that improvements in this area alone will suffice.

To illustrate this, in Exhibit 5 we compare Puerto Rico to three of the U.S. mainland's lowest-rated states: Pennsylvania, New Jersey and Illinois.

Exhibit 5: Puerto Rico's Debt Is Higher Than Lower-Rated U.S. States

	Pennsylvania	New Jersey	Illinois	Puerto Rico
Debt	$14.3 B	$37.0 B	$34.5 B	$55.5 B
Unfunded Pension Liabilities	$20.6 B	$37.3 B	$111.0 B	$43.6 B
Personal Income	$358.0 B	$313.4 B	$375.2 B	$38.2 B
GDP	$662.9 B	$549.1 B	$745.9 B	$103.1 B
Debt and Pensions-to-GDP Ratio	5.3%	13.5%	19.5%	96.1%
Debt and Pensions-to-Personal Income Ratio	9.7%	23.7%	38.8%	259.6%

Sources: Comprehensive Annual Financial Reports for Pennsylvania, New Jersey, Illinois and Puerto Rico; U.S. Census Bureau; Federal Reserve Bank of St. Louis.

As Exhibit 5 shows, Puerto Rico's debt and pension leverage is much greater than any of the lowest-rated mainland states, particularly in the context of each government's economic output and resident income. Simply increasing tax compliance will not reduce this over-leverage. Puerto Rico's real problem is indebtedness, not tax compliance.

This certainly does not mean that governmental reforms, expenditure cuts, improved tax compliance and collections, employee layoffs and government downsizing are not needed. Puerto Rico's budget projections will improve with greater austerity and fiscal discipline, but we still believe the magnitude of fixed costs outweighs the savings that can be achieved through cuts and efficiency improvements.

Moreover, with an outsized portion of Puerto Rico's employment derived from Commonwealth and local government employment (23.9% in Puerto Rico versus 13.5% for the mainland U.S.), extensive austerity will likely exacerbate the Commonwealth's economic contraction. We expect most creditors will continue to object to Governor García Padilla's plans to restructure Puerto Rico's debts, but our analysis continues to show that the territory's debts are unsustainable and require adjustment.

Finally, it is unclear whether a framework for the adjustment of state obligations through the federal court system would pass constitutional muster. Unlike Puerto Rico—a U.S. territory subject to the direct oversight of, and potential intervention by, Congress—states are sovereign entities with certain protections from federal interference specifically spelled out in the U.S. Constitution.

While legal opinions are mixed on this subject, many argue a federal bankruptcy regime for states wouldn't pass legal and constitutional muster because:

- Such a federal regime would violate principles of both state sovereignty and federalism.
- States opting to enter into any such hypothetical framework would necessarily be acting in direct violation of their own constitutions and/or contract laws.

Moreover, the sole instance of which we are aware of the U.S. government discharging state debt (according to a Fall 2011 *American Bankruptcy Law Journal* article) followed the civil war when the federal government nullified the debt issued by the former confederate states. This nullification occurred via a constitutional amendment specifically targeted to debt raised for the purposes of insurrection or rebellion against the United States. This implies there was no path to discharging the debt of U.S. states available through the balance of the U.S. Constitution.

In short, Puerto Rico accessing a Congressionally-approved restructuring regime is not a precursor to U.S. states following suit because:

- U.S. states, as sovereign entities, are likely constitutionally ineligible for federally supervised restructuring.
- U.S. states are significantly financially healthier than Puerto Rico and have far greater revenue flexibility, both in terms of rate headroom and the wealth and scope of their economies.
- Aside from not needing a federal restructuring regime, U.S. states have shown no inclination to ask for any such legislation and would likely oppose it.

Swift Action Will Help Build Confidence

We believe the best outcome is for the Puerto Rico situation to be resolved as quickly as possible. The faster the Puerto Rican government is forced to implement much needed structural reform and fiscal discipline, the earlier traditional institutional investors will view Puerto Rico as a defensible investment. Puerto Rico must show it can achieve and maintain financial discipline and an affordable debt structure to regain access to affordable and sustainable lending for infrastructure investment.

As a U.S. territory, Puerto Rico is not a true sovereign. It may be state-like, and there are good arguments for the Commonwealth to receive federal funding on parity with other states. However, as a territory it does not enjoy the same responsibilities and advantages as states. Puerto Rico is a sub-sovereign entity over which the U.S. Congress has oversight. When warranted, Congress should act to resolve various financial, economic and/or humanitarian crises within the territories.

Years of litigation and inter-creditor disputes will only stifle economic growth and accelerate out-migration, further diminishing the tax base available to pay off creditors. At present, too many unknowns prevent investors from reaching a reasonable degree of confidence in the territory or any particular security pledge. This lack of certainty will keep Puerto Rico locked out of the market until a path to sustainability and economic growth emerges. We believe this will not happen until

Congress enters the void and brings with them a sense of order and path forward for Puerto Rico.

———

The CHAIRMAN. Thank you. You are supposed to end with, "It's a good bill." I got it. OK.

Mr. Kent.

STATEMENT OF ANDREW KENT, PROFESSOR OF LAW, FORDHAM UNIVERSITY SCHOOL OF LAW, NEW YORK, NEW YORK

Mr. KENT. Thank you, Chairman Bishop, Ranking Member Grijalva, and distinguished members of the committee. I appreciate the invitation to testify today.

As you noted, I am a Professor of Law at Fordham University School of Law, and I teach constitutional law and other topics. I will comment briefly on the constitutional power of Congress to enact the proposed legislation.

As might be expected, almost all legislation coming from the Congress that deals with insolvency, restructuring, bankruptcy, and like topics is enacted under the bankruptcy clause of Article I. That clause provides that Congress shall have the power to establish uniform laws on the subject of bankruptcies throughout the United States.

The uniformity that this requires has been called by the Supreme Court "geographic uniformity," but, nevertheless, the Supreme Court has also indicated that the uniformity requirement is not a straitjacket, and it has in many different cases found that differences in the law and the way it applies to different classes of debtors and creditors are not violations of the uniformity requirement.

Congress may address geographically isolated problems under the bankruptcy clause without violating the uniformity requirement. And, as I said, Congress may treat different classes of debtors and creditors differently without violating the uniformity requirement.

Because this is a territory-specific law that deals with an entire class of debtors and is dealing with a geographically isolated problem, I think there are strong arguments that Congress could, if it wanted to, enact this under the bankruptcy clause without violating uniformity requirements.

But there would be some risks if that were the only basis under which Congress could act. Thankfully, it is not. There is another basis on which Congress can enact this legislation, and that is the so-called territorial clause of Article IV of the Constitution, the clause that is referenced in the new draft legislation in section 101. That clause empowers the Congress to make, "all needful rules and regulations respecting the territory or other property belonging to the United States."

Congress' power to use this clause to legislate for the territories has been called an absolute and undisputed power by Chief Justice John Marshall. Congress has well established and very long exercised power under this clause to treat territories differently from each other and to treat territories differently than it treats the states of the Union. And, in my judgment, this clause serves as an independent and sufficient basis with which Congress could enact the contemplated legislation.

The power of Congress under the territorial clause is vastly different than the power it has when it is legislating for states of the Union. Congress' power is limited when legislating for the states to certain enumerated or implied topics of national concern, but when legislating for the territories, Congress is given additional power by this clause—broad, general legislative powers that the Supreme Court has repeatedly analogized to those powers held by a state legislature.

So Congress, in fact, possesses two types of powers under this territorial clause. As the Supreme Court has said, the Nation possesses the sovereign powers of the general government, and it added to that when it is legislating in the territories, it also has the powers of a local or state government.

The Supreme Court has called this power "broad," "plenary," and even "practically unlimited." And the Supreme Court has numerous times emphasized that the interpretation of Congress' power to legislate for the territories must be flexible to allow Congress the flexibility that is needed to legislate in a practical and workable manner for the different situations of the different territories.

And, in fact, the history of congressional regulation of the territories has been one of tailoring legislation to the specific historical, geographic, economic, legal, and political conditions of the different territories. The history has also shown that Congress repeatedly uses the territorial clause to enact a wide array of legislation that it could not have enacted if it were legislating for the states under its Article I powers. My written testimony gives many examples of this.

There are actually three identically worded uniformity clauses in the Constitution. In addition to the bankruptcy uniformity clause, there is a requirement that imposts and excise taxes be uniform. The Supreme Court held as long ago as 1901 that that uniformity requirement—again, identically worded to the one in the bankruptcy clause—does not apply to Puerto Rico.

There is also a requirement of naturalization uniformity, again, with the exact same language as in the bankruptcy clause. The Supreme Court has not ruled on that, but the Courts of Appeals have held that naturalization uniformity does not apply in the unincorporated territories, such as Puerto Rico, and there is a very long history of congressional naturalization legislation that is disuniform, that treats the residents of territories very differently, without constitutional infirmity in that being found.

So, in a general matter, Congress only needs one constitutional basis upon which to enact legislation, and since I believe the territorial clause is sufficient for that, uniformity issues under the bankruptcy clause need not be raised.

Thank you very much.

[The prepared statement of Mr. Kent follows:]

PREPARED STATEMENT OF ANDREW KENT, PROFESSOR OF LAW, FORDHAM UNIVERSITY SCHOOL OF LAW, NEW YORK, NEW YORK

Chairman Bishop, Ranking Member Grijalva, and distinguished members of the committee, thank you for inviting me to testify today. I am a professor of law at

Fordham University School of Law, where I teach constitutional law and other topics.

As I understand the new draft legislation just released publicly, Title I creates a Financial Oversight and Management Board for Puerto Rico, and gives the legislatures of other U.S. territories the option to choose to have such an oversight board created for them. Title II sets out the responsibilities of any oversight board created under Title I. Title III, section 302, allows a U.S. territory or territorial instrumentality to be a debtor and follow specified debt adjustment procedures if it is subject to an oversight board created under Title I, that board has allowed the territory or territorial instrumentality to enter into a debt adjustment process, and the territory "desires to effect a plan to adjust its debts."

I. THE UNIFORMITY REQUIREMENT OF THE CONSTITUTION'S BANKRUPTCY CLAUSE

The Constitution's Bankruptcy Clause provides that "The Congress shall have power to . . . establish . . . uniform laws on the subject of bankruptcies throughout the United States." U.S. Const., art. I, § 8, cl. 4. Case law about this uniformity requirement establishes that, although it requires what the Supreme Court calls geographic uniformity, the clause nevertheless grants Congress great leeway. "The uniformity requirement is not a straitjacket . . . ." *Railway Labor Executives' Ass'n v. Gibbons*, 455 U.S. 457, 469 (1982). Congress may treat different classes of debtors differently; may incorporate state law in ways that will lead to different results in different states; and may address geographically isolated problems as long as the law operates uniformly on a given class of debtors and creditors. *See id.* at 465–69; *Blanchette v. Connecticut General Ins. Corp.*, 419 U.S. 102, 156–61 (1974); *Schultz v. United States*, 529 F.3d 343, 350–52 (6th Cir. 2008). The Supreme Court has struck down a law as non-uniform, however, where it applied to only a single debtor, one named railroad company. *See Railway Labor Executives' Ass'n*, 455 U.S. at 465–69.

In light of this case law, a question might be raised about whether the draft legislation could be subject to challenge for non-uniformity. The fact that legislation concerns debt adjustment for certain classes of debtors only—territories and territorial instrumentalities—is unlikely to be deemed objectionable under the Bankruptcy Clause uniformity provision. The Supreme Court has held that Congress may treat different classes of debtors differently. But to the extent that the legislation singles out Puerto Rico (and its instrumentalities), because only Puerto Rico has an oversight board created for it by the bill, uniformity questions might be raised.

Nevertheless, my view is that these constitutional concerns can be avoided in this case, because Congress may enact debt adjustment legislation for Puerto Rico under a different clause of the Constitution, a clause that does not require uniformity. That clause is the Territories or Territorial Clause of Article IV, as referenced in § 101(b)(3) of the new draft of the bill (setting out the "Constitutional Basis").

II. THE TERRITORIES CLAUSE ALLOWS NON-UNIFORM LEGISLATION

The Constitution empowers Congress to "make all needful rules and regulations respecting the territory or other property belonging to the United States." U.S. Const., art. IV, § 3. Congress' power to use this clause to make rules for the territories has been called an "absolute and undisputed power," by Chief Justice John Marshall. *Sere v. Pitot*, 10 U.S. 332, 336–37 (1810).

Congress has well-established and long-exercised power under this clause to treat territories differently from each other, and to treat territories differently than it treats U.S. states. In my judgment, this clause serves as an independent and sufficient basis on which Congress may enact the contemplated legislation. The remainder of my testimony will concern the Territorial Clause and the non-uniformity that it allows.

The power of Congress over the territories is vastly different than its power over the States of the Union. Congress' power is limited in legislating for the states to certain enumerated or implied topics of national concern. But when legislating for the territories, Congress is given additional power by the Territorial Clause—broad, general legislative power that the Supreme Court analogizes to that of a state legislature. *See, e.g., First Nat. Bank v. Yankton Cty.*, 101 U.S. 129, 133 (1879); *Benner v. Porter*, 50 U.S. 235, 242 (1850). Over a territory or dependency "the nation possesses the sovereign powers of the general government plus the powers of a local or a state government in all cases where legislation is possible." *Cincinnati Soap Co. v. United States*, 301 U.S. 308, 317 (1937). Thus, "[t]he powers vested in Congress by" the Territorial Clause "to govern Territories are broad," *Examining Bd. of Engineers, Architects, & Surveyors v. Flores de Otero*, 426 U.S. 572, 586 n.16

(1976), "plenary," *Binns v. United States*, 194 U.S. 486, 491 (1904), and even "practically unlimited," *Cincinnati Soap Co.*, 301 U.S. at 317.

The Supreme Court has many times emphasized that interpretation of Congress' ability to legislate for the territories under the Constitution must be marked by "flexibility," *Cincinnati Soap Co.*, 301 U.S. at 318, and concern for Congress's practical ability to govern, *see Torres v. Commonwealth of Puerto Rico*, 442 U.S. 465, 470 (1979).

Puerto Rico, though it is now formally a commonwealth, is still a territory of the United States within the meaning of the Territorial Clause. *See Torres*, 442 U.S. at 468–70; *Dávila-Pérez v. Lockheed Martin Corp.*, 202 F.3d 464, 468–69 (1st Cir. 2000); *Americana of Puerto Rico, Inc. v. Kaplus*, 368 F.2d 431, 435 (3d Cir. 1966). In other words, Congress may still today legislate for Puerto Rico pursuant to it plenary power over territorial legislation.[1]

The history of congressional regulation of the territories has been one of tailoring legislation to the specific historical, geographic, economic, legal, and political conditions of each particular territory. The history has also shown Congress using the Territorial Clause to enact a wide array of legislation that it could not enact for the states under its Article I powers.

Congress' first territorial legislation—enacted in 1787 by the Confederation Congress, and re-enacted in 1789 by the first Congress organized under the new Constitution—shows this pattern. *See* Act of Aug. 7, 1789, ch. 8, 1 Stat. 50. This law, the famous Northwest Ordinance, announced many rules that would apply only in the Northwest Territory. For example, it announced rules concerning intestate succession and conveyance of real estate, but then also provided that "the French and Canadian inhabitants" of the territory could continue to be governed by their own "laws and customs now in force among them." An Ordinance for the Government of the Territory of the United States Northwest of the River Ohio § 2 (July 13, 1787).

Many other examples could be given of congressional legislation that (1) could not have been enacted under Article I to apply in the states and (2) applied to one territory only and provided specifically tailored rules for that territory. After the Louisiana Purchase, Congress' legislation under the Territorial Clause provided special rules for that territory concerning the port of New Orleans. *See* Act of Feb. 24, 1804, ch. 13, §§ 6 & 8, 2 Stat. 251, 253. After the United States acquired Florida from Spain, Congress enacted specific rules regarding revenue collection for Spanish vessels trading with Florida. *See* Act of March 3, 1821, ch. 39, § 2, 3 Stat. 637, 639. When Congress organized the Territory of Oklahoma, it provided that certain specified chapters of the laws of the state of Nebraska would apply there, concerning mortgages, corporations, railroads, real estate, and other topics. *See* Act of May 2, 1890, ch. 182, § 11, 26 Stat. 81, 87. After the United States annexed Hawaii, Congress imposed caps on the amount of real estate that corporations could purchase in that territory only. *See* Act of April 30, 1900, ch. 339, § 55, 31 Stat. 141, 150. After the Philippines became a U.S. territory through the 1898 Treaty of Paris, Congress enacted a detailed set of provisions to govern mining and mining claims in that territory only. *See* Act of July 1, 1902, ch. 1369, §§ 20–50, 31 Stat. 691, 697–704.

Early on Congress recognized the utility of extending many general laws of the United States over the territories, but also recognized that not all laws applicable in the states would work well in some or all territories. As a result, Congress developed a practice of providing in the organic acts for territories that "all laws of the United States which are not locally inapplicable" shall apply in the territory. Act of Sept. 9, 1850, ch. 49, § 17, 9 Stat. 446, 452 (Territory of New Mexico). *See also* Act of March 3, 1863, ch. 117, § 13, 12 Stat. 808, 813 (Territory of Idaho); Act of May 26, 1864, ch. 95, § 13, 13 Stat. 85, 91 (Territory of Montana). This statutory provision was, in effect, a delegation from Congress to the courts to tailor the legislation of the United States to the specific local requirements of each organized territory. The ubiquity of these provisions, and the lack of successful constitutional challenges to them, evidences Congress' plenary authority to tailor legislation to the needs and circumstances of an individual territory.

The Supreme Court took up Congress' direction to determine which general laws were locally applicable or inapplicable in specific territories. When Congress specified in a statute that it would apply to "territories" as well as states, the Supreme Court examined "the character and aim of the act" to determine if a particular territory was covered. *People of Puerto Rico v. Shell Co.*, 302 U.S. 253, 258 (1937).

---

[1] *See also Cincinnati Soap Co.*, 301 U.S. at 319 (holding that Congress' legislative power over the Philippines under the Territorial Clause had not changed as a result of "the adoption and approval of a constitution for the Commonwealth of the Philippine Islands").

The Foraker Act, the organic act for Puerto Rico passed in 1900, contained this same "not locally inapplicable" tailoring provision, and specified also that Congress' internal revenue laws would not apply. *See* Act of April 12, 1900, ch. 191, § 14, 31 Stat. 77, 80.[2] Congress further tailored legislation specifically for Puerto Rico by also specifying in the Foraker Act that preexisting laws from the period of Spanish rule would continue in force unless they were repealed by the United States, in conflict with U.S. statutes, or determined to be "locally inapplicable." *Id.* § 8.

Congress enacted the "not locally inapplicable" provision only for so-called organized territories, *see* Revised Statutes § 1891 (1878),[3] in which Congress had created a local territorial government. Thus, Congress allowed even greater dis-uniformity in unorganized territories, where general rules of the United States were not extended by any such provision. Even within organized territories, Congress drew distinctions. When Congress organized a government for the Philippines, it provided that § 1891 did not apply, *see* Act of July 1, 1902, ch. 1369, § 1, 31 Stat. 691, 692, indicating an intent that generally applicable U.S. laws would not automatically extend to the Philippines.

In the Insular Cases, the Supreme Court held that the Constitution does not apply in full in so-called unincorporated territories, among which the Court included Puerto Rico and the Philippines. There are "inherent practical difficulties" with "enforcing all constitutional provisions 'always and everywhere.'" *Boumediene v. Bush*, 553 U.S. 723, 759 (2008). Thus under the Insular Cases, not all structural limitations on congressional power apply to territorial legislation, *see Torres*, 442 U.S. at 468–69, and "[o]nly 'fundamental' constitutional rights are guaranteed to inhabitants of those [unincorporated] territories," *United States v. Verdugo-Urquidez*, 494 U.S. 259, 268 (1990). Congressional legislation for an "unincorporated territory" like Puerto Rico is "not subject to all the provisions of the Constitution." *Torres*, 442 U.S. at 469. "In exercising this power [under the Territories Clause], Congress is not subject to the same constitutional limitations as when it is legislating for the United States." *Hooven & Allison Co. v. Evatt*, 324 U.S. 652, 674 (1945).[4]

In contrast to its allowance of flexibility and heterogeneity with territorial legislation, the Constitution prescribes a certain amount of uniformity when Congress is legislating for the States of the Union. Territorial legislation has sometimes been challenged on the grounds that it is dis-uniform and hence unconstitutional, but these challenges have not succeeded.

The Constitution specifies that three kinds of legislation should be "uniform" "throughout the United States": naturalization legislation, bankruptcy legislation, and certain taxes ("duties, imposts and excises").[5] Notwithstanding these clauses, it is well-established that naturalization and tax legislation for the territories need not be uniform—either with respect to legislation for States of the Union or with respect to legislation for other territories. It stands to reason that the Bankruptcy Clause, employing identical language about uniformity, also does not bind Congress when it legislates for the territories.

Tax uniformity not required for the territories: The Supreme Court held, in the Insular Cases, that Congress was not bound by the uniformity provision with regard to taxation when it enacted special revenue laws applying only to Puerto Rico. As the Court later summarized the rule:

> "In *Downes v. Bidwell*, 182 U.S. 244 (1901), we held that Congress could establish a special tariff on goods imported from Puerto Rico to the United States, and that the requirement that all taxes and duties imposed by

---

[2] Today 48 U.S.C. § 734 provides: "The statutory laws of the United States not locally inapplicable, except as hereinbefore or hereinafter otherwise provided, shall have the same force and effect in Puerto Rico as in the United States, except the internal revenue laws other than those contained in the Philippine Trade Act of 1946 [22 U.S.C.A. § 1251 et seq.] or the Philippine Trade Agreement Revision Act of 1955 [22 U.S.C.A. § 1371 et seq.]: *Provided, however,* That after May 1, 1946, all taxes collected under the internal revenue laws of the United States on articles produced in Puerto Rico and transported to the United States, or consumed in the island shall be covered into the Treasury of Puerto Rico."

[3] This statute provides: "The Constitution and all laws of the United States which are not locally inapplicable shall have the same force and effect within all the organized Territories, and in every Territory hereafter organized as elsewhere within the United States."

[4] *Hooven & Allison* was overruled in part on other grounds in *Limbach v. Hooven & Allison Co.*, 466 U.S. 353 (1984).

[5] *See* U.S. Const., art. I, § 8, cl. 1 ("The Congress shall have power to lay and collect taxes, duties, imposts and excises, to pay the debts and provide for the common defense and general welfare of the United States; but all duties, imposts and excises shall be uniform throughout the United States."); *id.* § 8, cl. 4 ("The Congress shall have power to . . . establish a uniform rule of naturalization, and uniform laws on the subject of bankruptcies throughout the United States.").

Congress be uniform throughout the United States, Art. I, §8, cl. 1, was not applicable to the island." *Torres*, 442 U.S. at 468–69.

As *Torres* indicates, *Downes* is still good law on this point.

The tax uniformity requirement has also been held inapplicable with regard to incorporated territories. In organizing and incorporating the Alaska Territory, Congress "created no legislative body" for the territory and so "established a revenue system of its own, applicable alone to that territory." *Binns*, 194 U.S. at 492. The Supreme Court rejected a claim that these Alaska-specific license and excise taxes enacted by Congress were required to be "uniform" with those "throughout the United States." *Id.* at 487, 494–96. As the Court noted:

> "It must be remembered that Congress, in the government of the territories . . . has plenary power, save as controlled by the provisions of the Constitution; that the form of government it shall establish is not prescribed, and may not necessarily be the same in all the territories." *Id.* at 491.

Naturalization uniformity not required for the territories: The Supreme Court has held that under the Territorial Clause or the clause allowing Congress to admit new states into the union Congress can accomplish the naturalization of aliens located in certain territories and adjust their status to that of U.S. citizens. *See Boyd v. Nebraska ex rel. Thayer*, 143 U.S. 135, 164–66, 168–70 (1892). The Court quoted with approval a lower court decision that "denied that the only constitutional mode of becoming a citizen of the United States is naturalization by compliance with the uniform rules established by Congress." *Id.* at 165–66. The "plenary power of Congress over the territories" can be used to collectively naturalize specific groups of people on the terms that Congress determines. *Id.* at 169.

Congress has long exercised plenary authority to determine whether residents of insular territories should be made citizens or not, and has made distinctions between different territories. Hawaii, Puerto Rico, Guam, and the Philippines were all acquired by the United States in 1898, but Congress treated residents of the territories very differently for citizenship purposes. In 1900, citizenship was granted to essentially all Hawaiians. *See* Act of April 30, 1900, ch. 339, §4, 31 Stat. 141, 141. Not until 1917 did Congress confer U.S. citizenship on many residents of Puerto Rico. *See* Act of March 2, 1917, ch. 145, §5, 39 Stat. 951, 953. Congress waited until 1940 to comprehensively grant citizenship to residents of Puerto Rico. *See* Nationality Act of 1940, ch. 876, §202, 54 Stat. 1137, 1139. Not until 1950 did Congress extend citizenship to Guamanians. *See* Act of Aug. 1, 1950, ch. 512, §4(a), 64 Stat. 384, 384. And Congress never granted citizenship to residents of the Philippines en masse, *see Valmonte v. INS*, 136 F.3d 914, 916–17 (2d Cir. 1998), though they were eligible for naturalization if they came within the terms of generally applicable statutes, *see, e.g., Balzac v. Porto Rico*, 258 U.S. 298, 308 (1922). Samoa, which was acquired by the United States in 1900, has also seen its residents excluded from automatic U.S. citizenship. *See Tuaua v. United States*, 788 F.3d 300, 302 (D.C. Cir. 2015).

Recently the Ninth Circuit confirmed that the uniformity provision of the Naturalization Clause cannot be invoked by residents of unincorporated territories to challenge non-uniform congressional rules. *See Eche v. Holder*, 694 F.3d 1026, 1031 (9th Cir. 2012).

Other uniformity cases: When litigants from the territories have used individual rights provisions of the Constitution to challenge congressional legislation under the Territorial Clause for lack of uniformity, the Supreme Court has rejected these claims. For instance, when individual rights challenges have been raised to social benefits legislation that treated residents of Puerto Rico differently than residents of the states, the Supreme Court has held that Congress "may treat Puerto Rico differently from states so long as there is a rational basis for its actions." *Harris v. Rosario*, 446 U.S. 651, 651-52 (1980) (AFDC program, Fifth Amendment Due Process Clause challenge); *see also Califano v. Torres*, 435 U.S. 1, (1978) (per curiam) (SSI program) (holding that Congress could treat Puerto Rico differently without violating the constitutional right to travel "[s]o long as its judgments are rational, and not invidious"). This kind of rational basis review is exceedingly deferential to the government. *See, e.g., FCC v. Beach Commc'ns, Inc.*, 508 U.S. 307, 314–15 (1993).

III. CONCLUSIONS

As a general matter, Congress needs only one constitutional grant of power upon which to enact legislation. And if the legislation meets the requirements of one grant, it does not matter if other possibly applicable grants do not support the legislation. *See, e.g., United States v. Morrison*, 529 U.S. 598, 607, 619 (2000).

It is true that the Supreme Court has held that, although general principles governing the reach of the Commerce Clause would allow Congress to enact bankruptcy legislation on that basis, Congress should not be allowed to use the Commerce Clause "to enact nonuniform bankruptcy laws," because that "would eradicate from the Constitution a limitation on the power of Congress to enact bankruptcy laws." *Railway Labor Executives' Ass'n*, 455 U.S. at 468–69.

The Supreme Court was not addressing and did not consider legislation governing the territories when it made that statement, and the case law and legal principles discussed above suggest that the Court's concerns about an end run around limitations on congressional power should not apply to the situation at hand, where Congress could act under the Territorial Clause.

The Territorial Clause is not an end run around anything. It is a specially crafted constitutional power designed to allow Congress to flexibly address the myriad practical problems of governing the territories, and to tailor its legislation to the unique circumstances of each territory. In many ways, the entire point of the Territorial Clause is to allow Congress to do things that it cannot otherwise do under Article I. That is how the clause has been consistently used by Congress and interpreted by the Supreme Court over the centuries.

In my judgment, the newly released draft legislation is within Congress's power under the Territorial Clause, which is not limited by the uniformity requirement of the Bankruptcy Clause.

That conclusion is supported by the recent decision in *Franklin California Tax-Free Trust v. Puerto Rico*, 805 F.3d 322 (1st Cir. 2015), in which two judges of the First Circuit opined that Congress could enact debt adjustment legislation specifically for Puerto Rico under its plenary power under the Territorial Clause. *See id.* at 337. One judge disagreed with this conclusion, however. *See id.* at 346–48 (Torruella, J., concurring in judgment). The Supreme Court has granted cert in this case, *see Acosta-Febo v. Franklin California Tax-Free Trust*, 136 S. Ct. 582 (2015), but it is not generally thought that the Court's decision is likely to address Bankruptcy Clause uniformity issues.

Thank you again for the opportunity to testify about this bill.

*****

Supplementary Testimony from Mr. Kent

FORDHAM UNIVERSITY SCHOOL OF LAW
NEW YORK, NEW YORK

April 20, 2016

Hon. ROB BISHOP, *Chairman,*
House Committee on Natural Resources,
1324 Longworth House Office Building,
Washington, DC 20515.

Re: H.R. 4900, the Puerto Rico Oversight, Management, and Economic Stability Act (PROMESA)

DEAR CHAIRMAN BISHOP AND MEMBERS OF THE COMMITTEE:

Thank you for inviting me to testify on April 13, 2016 on the constitutionality of the new draft of the Puerto Rico Oversight, Management, and Economic Stability Act (PROMESA). As you know, current federal bankruptcy law does not provide either a voluntary or involuntary debt adjustment process for U.S. states or territories. PROMESA would create such a process for territories. At the hearing, questions were asked about whether a debt adjustment bill similar to PROMESA could be enacted for U.S. state governments. I was asked to submit a letter amplifying my testimony about that topic, in particular focusing on the Contracts Clause of the U.S. Constitution.

As I understood the thrust of several questions, there might be concern about whether a debt adjustment law for territories, such as the current draft of PROMESA, could create a precedent for a bankruptcy bill for states. The constitutional considerations regarding congressionally-authorized debt adjustment for territories, like Puerto Rico, and debt adjustment for U.S. states are starkly different. So different that, in my view, PROMESA would not create constitutional precedent for a debt adjustment statute for states.

Territories and states are fundamentally distinct in our constitutional system. "[U]nder our federal system, the States possess sovereignty concurrent with that of the Federal Government, subject only to limitations imposed by the Supremacy Clause." *Gregory v. Ashcroft*, 501 U.S. 452, 457 (1991) (quotation marks omitted). "[T]he preservation of the States, and the maintenance of their governments, are as much within the design and care of the Constitution as the preservation of the Union and the maintenance of the National government. The Constitution, in all its provisions, looks to an indestructible Union, composed of indestructible States." *Id.* (quoting *Texas v. White*, 7 Wall. 700, 725 (1869)).

State sovereignty limits Federal power in a variety of important ways. *See, e.g.,* U.S. Const., art. X ("The powers not delegated to the United States by the Constitution, nor prohibited by it to the states, are reserved to the states respectively, or to the people."); *id.* art. XI ("The judicial power of the United States shall not be construed to extend to any suit in law or equity, commenced or prosecuted against one of the United States by citizens of another state, or by citizens or subjects of any foreign state."). Congressional power, when legislating for the states of the union, is limited to certain enumerated and implied topics of national concern.

By contrast, the Constitution empowers Congress to "make all needful rules and regulations respecting the territory or other property belonging to the United States." U.S. Const., art. IV, §3. Unlike U.S. states, territories are not constitutional sovereigns whose existence, structure, and powers are protected from Federal infringement by the Constitution. Over a territory or dependency "the Nation possesses the sovereign powers of the general government plus the powers of a local or a state government in all cases where legislation is possible." *Cincinnati Soap Co. v. United States*, 301 U.S. 308, 317 (1937). Thus, "[t]he powers vested in Congress by" the Territorial Clause "to govern Territories are broad," *Examining Bd. of Engineers, Architects, & Surveyors v. Flores de Otero*, 426 U.S. 572, 586 n.16 (1976), "plenary," *Binns v. United States*, 194 U.S. 486, 491 (1904), and even "practically unlimited," *Cincinnati Soap Co.*, 301 U.S. at 317.

As my written testimony for the April 13, 2016 hearing indicates, I believe that Congress has authority under Territorial Clause of Article IV to enact the PROMESA bill. But if Congress acting under Article I powers were to amend the bankruptcy code to allow either voluntary or involuntary debt adjustment for U.S. states, very serious questions would be raised about constitutionality. I cannot say definitively that such a statutory scheme would be found unconstitutional—extant Supreme Court case law does not allow that kind of precision, and the membership of the Court will likely be changing in the next year or so—but there is certainly a great risk of unconstitutionality.

The first question would be whether Congress has enumerated or implied power to enact bankruptcy legislation for state governments. The Constitution's Bankruptcy Clause provides that "The Congress shall have power to . . . establish . . . uniform laws on the subject of bankruptcies throughout the United States." U.S. Const., art. I, §8, cl. 4. The Supreme Court has never been squarely confronted with the question whether this power allows bankruptcy legislation for state governments. Certainly we can say, though, that the members of the Founding generation who drafted and voted to adopt this language did not contemplate that Congress would be legislating with regard to state governments. *See* Emily D. Johnson & Ernest A. Young, *The Constitutional Law of State Debt*, 7 Duke J. Const. L. & Pub. Pol'y 117, 155–56 (2012); Thomas Moers Mayer, *State Sovereignty, State Bankruptcy, and a Reconsideration of Chapter 9*, 85 Am. Bankr. L.J. 363, 367 (2011). But even if the Bankruptcy Clause could not support such legislation, Congress arguably would find sufficient power under the Interstate Commerce and Necessary and Proper Clauses of Article I of the Constitution. *But cf. Railway Labor Executives' Ass'n v. Gibbons*, 455 U.S. 457 (1982) (holding that Congress cannot do an end run around the uniformity requirement of the Bankruptcy Clause by legislating under the Commerce Clause).

A second question is whether state bankruptcy legislation would violate the Tenth Amendment and related principles protecting state sovereignty. In the 1930s, the Supreme Court held that a 1934 Federal bankruptcy law for municipalities that allowed bankruptcy courts to impair the control of state governments over the fiscal affairs of their municipal subdivisions was not constitutional, *see Ashton v. Cameron*

County Water Improvement Dist. No. 1, 298 U.S. 513, 528–29 (1936); *id.* at 539 (Cardozo, J., dissenting), while the 1937 amendment that both required state consent and sufficiently protected state sovereignty was constitutional, *see United States v. Bekins*, 304 U.S. 27, 49–51 (1938).

These two decisions are widely understood to have suggested that, to pass constitutional muster, any Federal bankruptcy regime that would apply to states would need to meet two requirements: states would need to consent (the process would need to be entirely voluntary), and the statute would need to prevent Federal bankruptcy courts from undermining state autonomy and sovereignty over taxing, spending, and other core sovereign matters. *See, e.g.*, Michael E. McConnell, *Extending Bankruptcy Law to States*, in WHEN STATES GO BROKE: THE ORIGINS, CONTEXT, AND SOLUTIONS FOR THE AMERICAN STATES IN FISCAL CRISIS 229, 230 (Peter Conti-Brown & David A. Skeel, Jr., eds., Cambridge Univ. Press 2012); Mayer, *supra*, at 374–75.[1]

Ashton and *Bekins* thus suggest that a mandatory oversight authority for states—akin to that found in PROMESA—could be subject to fatal constitutional objections. *See* David A. Skeel, Jr., *States of Bankruptcy*, 79 U. Chi. L. Rev. 677, 731 (2012). But even a purely voluntary bankruptcy process that attempted to respect state sovereignty could run into constitutional problems under the Tenth Amendment and principles of state sovereignty articulated in *Ashton* and *Bekins*. First, "viewed realistically, state bankruptcy would cut deeply into the inherently sovereign powers of the statute over taxation and expenditure," transferring at least some control over those matters to a bankruptcy court. *See* McConnell, *supra*, at 233–34. In other words, it would be hard to design a process that in fact avoided all interference with a state's core fiscal functions.

Second, more recent Supreme Court case law raises questions about whether state consent could cure Tenth Amendment concerns about Federal impairments of state sovereignty via a bankruptcy regime. The "anti-commandeering" case law bars Congress from "require[ing] the states to govern according to Congress' instructions," *New York v. United States*, 505 U.S. 144, 162 (1992), even if the state consents, *see id.* at 180–82. Federal legislation that commands state legislatures to regulate according to Federal instructions disrupts the accountability of local officials to their local electorates and hence undermines the constitutional plan. *See id.* at 168–69. The Supreme Court has also reiterated that constitutional limits on Federal action arising from federalism concerns and the Tenth Amendment protect structural interests and individual liberty, not just state sovereignty, *see, e.g., id.* at 181–82; *Bond v. United States*, 131 S. Ct. 2355, 2364 (2011), casting further doubt on whether state consent could cure an otherwise unwarranted invasion of state sovereignty. *See* McConnell, *supra*, at 234–35. If state consent is not effective, it is possible that even purely voluntary state bankruptcy would be unconstitutional, to the extent that it impaired the sovereignty and autonomy of state governments.

A third and final question is whether the Constitution would prohibit the impairment of state government contracts—for example, with bondholders—through a Federal debt adjustment process overseen by a bankruptcy court. The Contracts Clause provides that "No State shall . . . pass any . . . law impairing the obligation of contracts." U.S. Const., art. I, § 10, cl. 1. It might be said that no Contracts Clause problem would be posed by a congressional statute authorizing state bankruptcy, *see* Steven L. Schwarcz, *A Minimalist Approach to State "Bankruptcy,"* 59 U.C.L.A. L. Rev. 322, 337 (2011), because the Federal Government is not covered by the Contracts Clause, which expressly applies to "State[s]" only, *see Hanover Nat'l Bank v. Moyses*, 186 U.S. 181, 188 (1902). But if Tenth Amendment concerns, discussed above, require that the state consent to the Federal bankruptcy process and to any court orders stemming from it, then it would not only be Congress but arguably the state also that would be choosing and authorizing actions that impaired state contracts. Thus the Contracts Clause could come into play.

The Supreme Court's 1930s cases about municipal bankruptcy and state sovereignty do not answer all questions about the Contracts Clause as applied to a hypothetical statute authorizing state bankruptcy. The *Ashton* decision, about the 1934 law, suggested that states would violate the Contracts Clause by consenting

---

[1] Federal bankruptcy for states without state consent might also be unconstitutional under the Eleventh Amendment and principles of state sovereign immunity. The Supreme Court has not directly answered this question, and its case law has given inconsistent signals. *Compare Seminole Tribe v. Florida*, 517 U.S. 44 (1996) (holding that Congress may not abrogate state sovereign immunity under Article I powers) *and Central Virginia Community College v. Katz*, 546 U.S. 356 (2006) (holding that state sovereign immunity did not bar a bankruptcy court from voiding a preferential transfer from a private debtor to a state instrumentality). *See generally* Johnson & Young, *supra*, at 159–60; Mayer, *supra*, at 368.

to a congressional bankruptcy scheme that impaired state contractual obligations. *See* 298 U.S. at 531. But *Bekins*, the subsequent decision about a very similar statute, the 1937 amendment, did not discuss any Contracts Clause issues, perhaps suggesting that the Supreme Court had *sub silentio* reversed itself on the issue.

Under modern Contracts Clause jurisprudence, "impairment of a state's own contracts would face more stringent examination . . . than would laws regulating contractual relationships between private parties." *Allied Structural Steel Co. v. Spannaus*, 438 U.S. 234, 244 n.15 (1978). State laws regulating existing contractual relations must have "a legitimate public purpose. A state could not adopt as its policy the repudiation of debts. . . ." *United States Trust Co. of New York v. New Jersey*, 431 U.S. 1, 22 (1977) (quotation marks omitted). The courts must guard against "the state's self-interest" leading it to abuse contracting partners. *Id.* at 26. Impairments of contract rights must be "reasonable and necessary to serve an important public purpose." *Id.* at 25. The greater and more permanent the impairment to contract rights, the less likely it is to be constitutional. *See, e.g., Home Building & Loan Ass'n v. Blaisdell*, 290 U.S. 398, 425, 430, 433, 441 (1934). Similarly, if contract rights were more theoretical than real to begin with, a subsequent impairment by the state is less likely to be proscribed by the Constitution. *See Faitoute Iron & Steel Co. v. city of Asbury Park*, 316 U.S. 502, 510–13 (1942) (holding that bondholders' ability to sue defaulting municipalities under preexisting law was an empty "right to pursue a sterile litigation" and the challenged state law allowing municipal debt restructuring did not violate the Contracts Clause).

It cannot be predicted with certainty how voluntary state bankruptcy allowed by a congressional statute would be treated under the Contracts Clause by the Supreme Court applying the doctrines described above. A lot could depend on details—for instance, did the bankruptcy process impose significant "haircuts" on the principal owed to bondholders, or did it merely extend the payment period by a reasonably short amount of time. The former would be more likely unconstitutional than the latter.

The Supreme Court's case law under the Fifth Amendment also protects against impairment of contract rights. "The Supreme Court has made clear that retroactive legislation that affects valid property interests raises problems under both" the Takings Clause and the Due Process Clause of the Fifth Amendment. Johnson & Young, *supra*, at 144 (discussing *Eastern Enterprises v. Apfel*, 524 U.S. 498 (1998)). As with the Contracts Clause, it is uncertain how a hypothetical congressional statute for state bankruptcy would fare under the Fifth Amendment, and the outcome of judicial review would depend significantly on the particular details of the legislation and any challenged court orders issued pursuant to it.

In sum, a congressional statute allowing state government bankruptcy would raise a number of serious constitutional issues, implicating unsettled areas of Supreme Court doctrine. In my judgment, there is a real risk that either the legislation itself or particular applications of it by bankruptcy courts would be found unconstitutional. By contrast, as my April 13 testimony indicated, I believe that PROMESA rests on a firm constitutional foundation.

Sincerely,

ANDREW KENT, PROFESSOR OF LAW
Fordham University School of Law.

————

The CHAIRMAN. Thank you.
Next, Mr. Kirpalani.

STATEMENT OF SUSHEEL KIRPALANI, PARTNER, QUINN EMANUEL URQUAHART & SULLIVAN, NEW YORK, NEW YORK

Mr. KIRPALANI. Thank you, Chairman Bishop, Ranking Member Grijalva, and members of the committee, as well as your dedicated staff, who have worked many nights and weekends to get us to this place. Thank you for having me participate in this important issue for our country. It is truly an honor to be here.

My name is Susheel Kirpalani. I am a partner at Quinn Emanuel in New York, and I am a creditors' rights lawyer. I am here to testify about fair restructuring laws and principles and whether the bill for Puerto Rico has the hallmarks of fairness and upholding the rule of law consistent with U.S. precedent.

I have been practicing creditors' advocacy for over 20 years. I represented creditors in the two largest municipal bankruptcy cases in the United States—Jefferson County, Alabama, and Detroit, Michigan. I have also represented the largest statutory creditors committees in Chapter 11 cases in the Lehman and Enron bankruptcies. I also served as a court-appointed mediator trying to solve myriad disputes among stakeholders in a multi-billion-dollar case.

Here, I represent COFINA creditors. COFINA is the largest bond issuer in Puerto Rico. When you think about Puerto Rico and you hear numbers like $70 billion of borrowed-money debt and $40 billion of pension debt, out of the $70 billion, COFINA is $17 billion. If you take out the utilities, you are left with $40 billion of borrowed-money debt apart from the utilities, the electric power, and the water system. So, $17 billion out of $40 billion is COFINA. It is the largest issuer of bonds in Puerto Rico, and they are secured creditors protected by property rights under both the U.S. Constitution and the Puerto Rico Constitution.

My clients include individuals who are retired or semi-retired as well as asset managers that invested in these safest, most secure bonds. This is how we are different from other bondholders: we are backed by the sales taxes of Puerto Rico. So, although creditors like the ones I represent certainly want to see their debts repaid, our interests are aligned with the people of Puerto Rico, because if they cannot afford to go out every day and buy things they need for their families, we can never get repaid. And if they leave home and move to the mainland states, we can never get repaid. So, our interests are truly aligned.

There are universal principles of any fair restructuring law: stay litigation, uphold creditor expectations, uphold the rule of law, and protect property rights as determined by the local law. If we want to stabilize Puerto Rico under U.S. principles, you need to respect U.S. traditions. This is not Greece. We have our own rules based on 100 years of Supreme Court jurisprudence.

My wife loves a show called "MythBusters." I don't know if anybody has seen that, but there are two myths that I would like to dispel today. The first, which I have seen on television—I am sure some of you have seen that or your families have seen that—that this is a bailout. This is not a bailout. This involves no U.S. taxpayer money, this bill. The second one is that this is "Super Chapter 9." I have a lot of experience with Chapter 9. This is no Chapter 9.

The problem with Chapter 9 is the law allows the local government to retain absolute control over its finances, its revenues, and its decisionmaking on which debts to pay and which debts not to pay. So, if you think about it, a local government is usually going to try to respect its electorate and the local interests, which is harmful to the municipal bond market. The difference here, of course, is the control board, and that difference is quite significant and makes it absolutely immune from being confused with Chapter 9.

This bill is the right framework for debt-restructuring laws under U.S. traditions and, critically, it will actually encourage voluntary agreements by creditors. We have gone on record publicly supporting Chairman Bishop's efforts, as well as the efforts of House leadership. Other creditors have not.

We actually have no problems with other creditors, whether they are general obligations creditors or the lowest tier of unsecured bondholders of the Commonwealth, but some of those creditors have regrettably engaged in negative advertising just to obstruct you from trying to do this very difficult job.

We think this is the right bill, and we appreciate the opportunity to answer any questions that you might have.

Thank you.

[The prepared statement of Susheel Kirpalani follows:]

PREPARED STATEMENT OF SUSHEEL KIRPALANI, PARTNER, QUINN EMANUEL URQUAHART & SULLIVAN, NEW YORK, NEW YORK

Thank you for inviting me to testify on the bill proposed by Chairman Bishop for bespoke legislation needed to address Puerto Rico's financial crisis. I am honored to be here.

BACKGROUND

My name is Susheel Kirpalani. I am the Chairperson of the Bankruptcy and Restructuring Group at the law firm Quinn Emanuel Urquhart & Sullivan, LLP. For more than 20 years, I have practiced exclusively in the area of creditors' rights. Beginning in the late 1990s, I have primarily represented creditors in debt restructurings driven by unanticipated financial collapse, typically as a result of questionable accounting practices, lack of transparency in financial reporting, and over-leveraged balance sheets. These restructurings include: Enron Corporation; Refco Inc.; and Lehman Brothers. In each matter, I represented the statutory committee of unsecured creditors—a fiduciary body appointed by the bankruptcy division of the U.S. Department of Justice to protect creditor rights and priorities. In 2012, I was appointed to serve as the examiner and mediator for stakeholders of Dynegy Holdings, the Houston-based energy company that once tried to save Enron, and which filed for Chapter 11 with a "pre-arranged plan" that subverted creditor priorities.

I also have relevant experience from the two largest Chapter 9 bankruptcy cases in history—Jefferson County, Alabama and Detroit, Michigan. In Jefferson County, I spent over 3 years working with the largest insurer of sewer system bonds to successfully restructure and reduce the system's overblown debt load to match the ability of the citizens of Jefferson County to repay ballooning debts incurred by corrupt public officials.

With respect to Puerto Rico's financial crisis, for the past 10 months, I have been representing a coalition of creditors made up of retirees and individual investors as well as asset managers GoldenTree Asset Management LP, Merced Capital LP, Tilden Park Capital Management, Whitebox Advisors LLC, and others. These creditors invested primarily, if not exclusively, in the safest and most secure senior bond investment Puerto Rico offered known as COFINA.[1] COFINA is a Spanish-language acronym for the Puerto Rico Sales Tax Financing Corporation created at the outset of Puerto Rico's fiscal crisis in 2006, in the wake of the Commonwealth government's shutdown for 2 weeks, which left 500,000 school children without a place to study and over 100,000 public employees without pay.[2] COFINA was created to insulate creditors from the lack of transparency and political and credit risk relating to the Commonwealth's general fund.[3] Similar to other public and private bonds, COFINA is a form of securitization, in which a specific revenue stream is transferred or pledged to support bond issues by a separate legal entity. Securitizations

---

[1] See, e.g., Janney Fixed Income Strategy, June 29, 2010, available at http://www.janney.com/file%20library/muni%20sector%20scorecard/cofina%206-29-10.pdf ("COFINA is the strongest Puerto Rico issuer from a credit standpoint. The sales tax revenue bonds have a secure foundation, based on a broad based sales tax and a strong legal framework").

[2] Puerto Rico Closes Government Offices, Schools Amid Fiscal Crisis, USA Today, May 1, 2006, available at http://usatoday30.usatoday.com/news/nation/2006-05-01-puertorico_x.htm.

[3] Standard & Poor's, Puerto Rico Sales Tax Fin. Corp.; Sales Tax, May 18, 2009, at 2–3.

significantly reduce costs of borrowing money by separating a revenue stream from an entity's credit profile. Today, COFINA is the largest debt issuer in Puerto Rico, with approximately $17 billion of secured bonds outstanding, including more than $7 billion of senior bonds and more than $9 billion of subordinated bonds.

COFINA bonds—held by many U.S. retail investors and pension recipients—are supported by a dedicated sales and use tax protected under both the U.S. and Puerto Rico constitutions. Given that the revenues for COFINA are dependent on sales activity on island, COFINA bondholders want to help craft a solution to Puerto Rico's fiscal crisis that helps drive on-island commerce, empowers Puerto Rico's economy, and stops the population flight to the states.

THE NEED FOR FEDERAL LEGISLATION

Puerto Rico simply cannot pay all of its debts. The crippling debt service Puerto Rico heaped upon itself is suffocating the economy now a decade into recession. Young Puerto Ricans have figured out how to escape the debt burden, and are now migrating to the mainland United States in large numbers, accelerating the shrinkage of Puerto Rico's economy, and further concentrating the debt burden on the citizens and businesses that remain on the island. This is now forcing Puerto Rico to take ad hoc and extraordinary actions that abuse creditors' rights. Puerto Rico recently enacted a debt moratorium law that grants its governor absolute power to choose to pay or not pay any public debts. One of the three challenges made to the constitutionality of Puerto Rico's ability to enact restructuring legislation is currently before the U.S. Supreme Court. It can be anticipated that there will also be constitutional challenges to the debt moratorium law. I previously believed that the need for Congress to intervene was already evident, but it has become urgent if there is to be any hope of an orderly process that respects property rights and the rule of law, stems out-migration, restores Puerto Rico to health, and avoids the risk of a taxpayer-funded bailout down the road.

FAIR DEBT ADJUSTMENT LAWS

Title III of PROMESA is entitled "Adjustment of Debts." This title designs a set of rules that would apply to any impairment of rights of a creditor of Puerto Rico or any of its instrumentalities. Although not a part of Title 11 of the United States Code (the "Bankruptcy Code"), Title III of PROMESA borrows some battle-tested rules contained in the Bankruptcy Code, which were shaped by over 100 years of U.S. jurisprudence on the constitutional limits of Federal power over private rights. As such, these rules form the core of American creditor expectations in the event a borrower becomes unable to repay its debts.

The first step of understanding any restructuring regime is to ask which creditor claims will potentially be subject to adjustment. In recognition of the reality that most of the near-term strain on Puerto Rico is at the general fund level, Puerto Rico's own recently passed debt moratorium law applies to all issuers of public debt, including the Commonwealth itself. Moreover, Puerto Rico's general obligations or "GO" bondholders assert a superior right to be paid from resources available to the treasurer of Puerto Rico and maintained in the general fund of Puerto Rico before other public debts of the Commonwealth can be paid.[4] The extent of this priority has never been examined by the Supreme Court of Puerto Rico and resolution of that issue by agreement or adjudication will figure prominently in any adjustment of debts of the Commonwealth. Due to the competing claims of creditors from the same ultimate source of repayment—Puerto Rican taxpayers—any restructuring of Puerto Rico is a zero-sum game because the population's resources are limited and will be further limited if out-migration continues or economic growth does not resume.[5] In my experience representing creditors' committees in the largest Chapter 11 cases in history, and having served as a court-appointed mediator, I believe the only way to build a global consensual compromise free from challenge is for every stakeholder group to roll up their sleeves and participate in good-faith negotiations and, failing a voluntary agreement among all groups, to resolve the priority of competing creditor rights in a judicial proceeding. Artificially excluding significant creditor groups from a restructuring regime will lead to protracted litigation, constitutional challenges, and delays to finding a solution, which would only serve to destroy economic value on the whole, and exacerbate creditor losses.

---

[4] Puerto Rico Const., Art. VI, § 8.

[5] For a quick thumbnail on the reasons for Puerto Rico's fiscal crisis, see Michelle Kaske and Martin Z. Braun, Puerto Rico's Slide, April 6, 2016, *available at* http://www.bloombergview.com/quicktake/puerto-ricos-slide.

Fundamental to U.S. creditors' rights law is the provision of a "breathing spell" for the debtor that cannot pay—in the form of an automatic stay of creditor enforcement actions—followed by a "discharge" or "fresh start" while respecting creditor priorities and ensuring property rights are not taken for the greater good without just compensation. In reality, this stay of creditor rights actually may enhance creditor recoveries by (1) removing the ability to race to the courthouse and obtain preferential treatment, which would otherwise favor well-heeled sophisticated institutions to the detriment of individuals and other creditors at large, and (2) allowing the beleaguered borrower to stabilize and rehabilitate its financial condition and future prospects without the resource drain and distraction of a rash of lawsuits. And if the debtor abuses the stay by, for example, failing to negotiate in good faith, creditors can seek to have the stay lifted.

The goals of any fair and effective restructuring regime should be to protect creditor expectations to the greatest extent practicable and to ensure any necessary taking of private property for public purposes is in exchange for just compensation. The means of achieving these goals are as follows: (1) restructure balance sheets and set budgets on a debtor-by-debtor basis; (2) establish classes of creditors in a fair and common-sense manner—in other words, insist that only "substantially similar" claims with similar legal and contractual rights against the same borrower are grouped together, fully recognizing the secured and priority status of some creditors; (3) solicit the votes of creditors in a fair way, consistent with due process of law including by providing adequate information to make a decision about any proposed adjustment; (4) treat each class of creditors according to its members' legal and contractual priorities, as determined by the local law governing the borrower and its relationship with creditors; and (5) ensure that a restructuring is in the "best interests of creditors" by mandating that creditors receive at least as much as they would have received in the absence of Federal intervention. Although the Bankruptcy Code has not always accomplished these strict goals, particularly in the context of municipal bankruptcy where the locality retains plenary and exclusive control over its finances and proposing a debt adjustment plan, the provisions of the Bankruptcy Code contain state-of-the-art rules that are the envy of much of the world's less-developed financial markets and legal systems.[6]

COLLECTIVE ACTION AND THE ABILITY TO BIND HOLDOUTS

It is a given that if unanimous consent by all stakeholders were required to confirm a debt adjustment plan, it would be impossible to ever achieve a voluntary compromise. For example, different people have different risk tolerance, a greater or lesser penchant for litigation, and some may prefer an expedient solution that minimizes cost but delivers recovery in the shortest amount of time. Accordingly, even the most "voluntary" of collective action rules recognize the need to bind holdouts who may otherwise seek to extract additional value for themselves even if it means risking value for all. So, it has been a constant feature of restructuring laws in the United States to permit the restructuring of an entire class of debt as long as a majority in number and two-thirds in dollar amount support the deal. This is not "cramdown," and is simply the American style of "collective action" within each specific class. PROMESA has this feature.

But the question occasionally arises when an entire class of creditors seeks to hold out for more than its members are legally entitled, and those creditors' unwillingness to accept their fair share prevents all other classes of creditors from moving forward. This rare scenario is when the "cramdown" rule found in section 1129(b) of the Bankruptcy Code must be invoked. I believe the ability to bind holdouts is a reasonable and necessary component of any effective restructuring authority. In my view, having the ability to bind holdouts if they engage in brinkmanship is the only way to get everyone to the table and have any hope of a voluntary agreement. It also promotes predictable outcomes, which is of paramount importance to creditors. Omitting this critical feature, which protects all other classes of creditors who do wish to voluntarily restructure their debts, would lead to unpredictable behavior and discourage consensual arrangements. It is tantamount, in other words, to handing a gun to junior creditors with which they can hold up senior creditors for value in excess of their legal rights or that which they could hope to achieve under current

---

[6] In the aftermath of Dubai's real estate crisis, in 2009, I was retained by the quasi-sovereign entity, Dubai World, to participate in the drafting of Dubai's first-ever restructuring law. Hopeful to restore confidence and credibility, it was the consensus among all involved that United States laws in this area achieved the best outcomes for creditors and, as a result, reestablishment of creditor confidence and market re-entry. Several features of U.S. law were borrowed in the enactment of Decree 57 of Dubai, which paved the way to achieve billions of dollars of relief through voluntary agreements with the backstop of a judicial system, only if needed.

law. Cramdown is a term of art for ensuring that creditor treatment complies with the "absolute priority" rule, a legal concept that has been a critical part of U.S. restructuring jurisprudence since at least the 1898 Bankruptcy Act. When used properly and in accordance with strict Congressional mandates, cramdown ensures the fairness of the restructuring process.

The National Bankruptcy Conference, a non-partisan organization of 60 of the Nation's leading bankruptcy scholars, recently had this to say about the "Discussion Draft" of PROMESA:

> The Conference believes that granting a Title III debtor the power to confirm a plan of adjustment over the rejection of the plan by an impaired class of creditors-including one comprising holders of bond debt-is critical to the success of a Title III case. *Without cramdown, Title III would provide a dissenting class with absolute veto power over a plan of adjustment.* The various protections afforded nonconsenting classes such as the prohibition against unfair discrimination as well as the incorporation of the absolute priority rule in sections 1129(b)(2)(A) and 1129(b)(2)(B), level the negotiation playing field, and should serve to encourage both sides to reach agreement, which is a stated goal of the House Committee on Natural Resources.[7]

THE PERILS OF CHAPTER 9 AND THE MYTH OF "SUPER CHAPTER 9"

Select bond investors have lobbied hard against PROMESA, including through the placement of targeted advertisements in members' districts, suggesting it is some form of "Super Chapter 9" because it incorporates provisions of the Bankruptcy Code. This is misleading and misguided. PROMESA is not an amendment to the Bankruptcy Code, and in fact implements significant changes from Chapter 9 that are specifically designed to ensure Federal oversight and the fair treatment of creditors. Nor could PROMESA's territory-specific provisions ever be "contagious" to the states. The reason is the Tenth Amendment of the U.S. Constitution. The Tenth Amendment is a recognition of our dual sovereign form of government—that it is the various states that created the Federal Government. By contrast, under the Territories Clause of the U.S. Constitution, the Federal Government has plenary authority to enact needful rules and regulations respecting the unincorporated territories.

Chapter 9 has led to failed creditor expectations because local, elected officials remain in control and can lawfully use the stay to prevent creditor enforcement while retaining discretion as to which debts to honor during the bankruptcy case. Moreover, the elected officials have exclusive authority to formulate a plan and could use that authority to favor local interests.[8] By the time the plan is presented to creditors, bondholders may have no choice but to cry uncle because they have no ability to force repayment and no recourse to an impartial decisionmaking body. All they can do at that late stage is object to the plan, vote against it, and hope the bankruptcy judge forces the debtor to go back to the drawing board. The inherent unfairness in that process is the necessary byproduct of balancing state sovereignty with the desire for Federal legislation to restructure a municipality's debts. The initial version of bankruptcy law designed by Congress for state municipalities in 1934 was held unconstitutional 2 years later as violating the Tenth Amendment.[9] The "sweeping character of the holding of the Supreme Court" called for a far lighter touch— one that offers debt adjustment tools to a municipality upon election by the state but on the condition that the state retained full control over all its municipality's political or governmental powers, and the Federal court was unable to interfere with

---

[7] Comments on the Discussion Draft of an Act Entitled "Puerto Rico Oversight, Management, and Economic Stability Act," *available at* http://newnbc.wpengine.com/wp-content/uploads/2015/07/2016-April-8-NBC-Statement-on-PROMESA.pdf (emphasis added).

[8] *See* Recent Municipal Bankruptcies Provide Greater Clarity on Outcomes for Investors, *Moody's Investor Services, Sector-In-Depth*, Feb. 25, 2016 ("Given the choice between cutting retiree liabilities (pensions and OPEBs) and [bond] debt, local governments may choose to impair debt more severely than pensions and OPEBs.").

[9] *See Ashton v. Cameron County*, 298 U.S. 513, 536 (1936) ("If obligations of states or their political subdivisions may be subjected to the interference here attempted, they are no longer free to manage their own affairs; the will of Congress prevails over them . . . And really the sovereignty of the state, so often declared necessary to the Federal system, does not exist.) (citing *McCulloch v. Maryland*, 4 Wheat. 316, 430).

a municipality's property and revenues. The revised statute was upheld by the Supreme Court [10] and is the predecessor to modern-day Chapter 9.

In stark contrast, PROMESA does not leave unfettered control over fiscal matters to the Governor and Legislative Assembly in Puerto Rico. Unconstrained by the Tenth Amendment because Puerto Rico is not a state, pursuant to the Territories Clause, PROMESA would install a non-political oversight board—which Congress will play a significant role in selecting—to ensure that local interests are not favored over long-distance creditors, and that decisions on issues of greatest concern to creditors are overseen and approved by a dispassionate, disinterested board. Significantly, only the oversight board would be able to propose a plan of adjustment for creditor vote and judicial approval. This is a profound difference with Chapter 9, in which it is the debtor that determines when to file.

Moreover, while Chapter 9 led to failed creditor expectations in the case of Detroit, commentators have correctly observed that the fault was not with the rules of the Bankruptcy Code as much as with the bankruptcy judge who generously interpreted its flexibility.[11] If applied correctly, the Bankruptcy Code "removes the risk that a debtor will pick and choose which obligations to pay, and it ensures that creditors' priorities will be honored."[12] The practicalities of Chapter 9—including the sovereignty point just discussed—make it inappropriate for Puerto Rico, particularly given the heavy interest of distant, state-side investors in Puerto Rican debt.

It is unclear whether PROMESA utilizes the Federal Bankruptcy Court system. There is a reference in section 306 of the bill to 28 U.S.C. § 157, which permits the District Courts to refer matters to bankruptcy judges, and in section 309 to 28 U.S.C. § 158(a), which governs appeals from Bankruptcy Courts. Bankruptcy judges serve for 14-year terms and derive their power from Article I of the Constitution. As such, they do not have life tenure and cannot without consent of the parties exercise the judicial power of the United States, except for certain "core bankruptcy" areas. Congress may want to consider whether an event as significant as a territorial restructuring, pursuant to the Territories Clause, should be heard by the Federal District Courts which exercise the judicial power of the United States pursuant to Article III of the Constitution. There may be issues that arise in a territorial restructuring that some creditors may challenge the Bankruptcy Court's power to hear and determine. Requiring that cases under Title III of PROMESA be heard in the District Court would further distinguish the regime from Chapter 9.

Unlike Chapter 9, the oversight board has authority to move the venue to a district outside the affected region if necessary.

PROVISIONS TO FURTHER PROTECT CREDITOR EXPECTATIONS AND RESPECT TERRITORIAL LAW

The rules for classifying only "substantially similar" claims together and ensuring a plan treats creditors "fairly and equitably" and does not "discriminate unfairly" are bedrock principles of American law. Given the potential for creative interpretation of those phrases, however, Congress should consider giving stricter definitional certainty to protect creditor expectations that the laws and agreements governing their claims will be respected and not tossed aside based on one judge's views of what is fair at the time. Imposing stricter definitional certainty would, with respect to Puerto Rico, make it impossible to classify GO bonds with inferior unsecured claims, such as pension claims or bonds that are subject to clawback, or to lump COFINA senior bonds together with contractually subordinate bonds. By setting the classification rules properly, only creditors with the same rights against the same issuer can be counted together and receive the same treatment. Further, especially given the lesson of Detroit, judicial restraint can be imposed by further defining the concepts of "fair and equitable" and whether discrimination is "unfair" based on creditor priorities found in the law or by agreement, not in the personal views of the jurist.

Another "must have" feature of any Federal law that prevents or otherwise impairs creditor rights is to ensure that—when all is said and done—every creditor fares no worse than they would have under current law, had the Federal case never

---

[10] *See United States v. Bekins*, 304 U.S. 27, 51 (1938) ("The [revised] statute is carefully drawn so as not to impinge upon the sovereignty of the state. The state retains control of its fiscal affairs.").

[11] David Skeel, Fixing Puerto Rico's Debt Mess, *The Wall St. Journal*, Jan. 5, 2016 ("[T]he rule of law took a beating in the Detroit bankruptcy . . . Steven Rhodes, the Federal bankruptcy judge in the Detroit case, instead concluded that the requirement was met as long as the plan satisfied his conscience").

[12] *Id.*

been commenced or were it to be dismissed. This is known as the "best interests of creditors" test and is one of the requirements to confirm a plan of adjustment under PROMESA. The "best interests" test also comes out of bankruptcy case law, and specifically ensures that the Federal Government will not be liable in eminent domain for "taking" property without just compensation because the creditor's recovery must be, by definition, at least as much as the creditor would have received had Federal legislation never intervened.[13] Greater definitional certainty could be included in PROMESA, again to make it more protective of individual creditors and to prevent courts from merely rubber stamping a proposed plan just because it is supported by the requisite majorities.

Finally, Federal courts overseeing bankruptcy cases are routinely called upon to address issues of state or territorial law, because it is those laws, not Federal, that defines property interests.[14] The uncertain determination of key issues affecting creditor recoveries is often a cause for concern among participants in a bankruptcy case. Any doubt over whether the Federal judge retains discretion to attempt to divine issues of first impression of Puerto Rican law bearing on constitutional or property interests of creditors should be removed under PROMESA. The law should require direct certification of such issues to the territorial high court, namely, the Supreme Court of Puerto Rico. This feature would not only promote and protect creditor expectations, which were set by local law, but would reduce the risk of undue Federal interference with insular territorial law and is consistent with U.S. Supreme Court jurisprudence.[15] The bill in its current form does not have any type of Federal court abstention, not even the type contained in 28 U.S.C. § 1334, which applies to bankruptcy cases. The original "discussion draft" contained an appropriate provision to require expedited determination by the territorial high court of issues of first impression under the territory's laws.

COLLECTIVE ACTION CLAUSES

I have been analyzing whether "Collective Action Clauses" or "CACs" could work for Puerto Rico. To be clear, CACs would *retroactively* change individual creditor rights, without judicial supervision and accepted notions of due process of law, so this raises many of the same constitutional concerns as bankruptcy without any precedent on which to rely. Special care must be taken to ensure any proposed modification is consistent with contractual and property rights among the competing creditors. While these types of provisions have been introduced in the Euro-Zone, they have never been a part of the fabric of American creditors' rights and they were not developed from the "takings" jurisprudence of the United States.[16] Title VI of the bill contains a mechanism for retroactively changing contract rights of bondholders through votes by two-thirds in amount of bonds in a given "pool." The bill thoughtfully includes careful classification rules and also ensures any modification meets the "best interests of creditors" test, both of which are critical. To be clear, these features are the minimum floor of creditors' rights, and additional features to protect against unfair results or improper motivations of creditors in overlapping pools may be appropriate. The CAC concept in Title VI, moreover, is only applicable to bond debt, which raises questions about overall fairness if only bonds will be subjected to compromise, and not other liabilities of Puerto Rico.

––––––––––

The CHAIRMAN. Thank you.
Mr. Johnson.

––––––––––

[13] *See Faitoute Iron & Steel Co. v. city of Asbury Park*, 316 U.S. 502, 515–16 (1942).

[14] *Butner v. United States*, 440 U.S. 48 (1979) ("Uniform treatment of property interests by both state and Federal courts within a state serves to reduce uncertainty, to discourage forum shopping, and to prevent a party from receiving 'a windfall merely by reason of the happenstance of bankruptcy.'") (citation omitted).

[15] Manuel Del Valle, Puerto Rico Before The United States Supreme Court, 19 Rev. Juridica U. Inter. P.R. 13 (1984) ("In the case of Puerto Rico, its economic, social and cultural development has been intimately associated with its legal development and ability to exercise insular sovereignty over matters of local concern.") (collecting SCOTUS cases that reversed the First Circuit Court of Appeals in deference to the Supreme Court of Puerto Rico on issues of Puerto Rican law).

[16] *See* Collective Action Clauses No Panacea for Sovereign Debt Restructurings, *available at* https://www.pimco.com/insights/viewpoints/viewpoints/collective-action-clauses-no-panacea-for-sovereign-debt-restructurings ("German Chancellor Angela Merkel and French President Nicolas Sarkozy, meeting in the French seaside resort of Deauville amid the escalating eurozone debt crisis in 2010, agreed to make them *de rigeuer* for sovereign bonds European countries issue under U.K. law from 2013.").

STATEMENT OF SIMON JOHNSON, PROFESSOR OF GLOBAL ECONOMICS AND MANAGEMENT, MIT SLOAN SCHOOL OF MANAGEMENT, CAMBRIDGE, MASSACHUSETTS

Dr. JOHNSON. Thank you, Mr. Chairman.

I would like to make three points. The first is on the nature of the debt crisis and the potentially severe consequences of not dealing with it.

I was previously Chief Economist at the International Monetary Fund. I have worked on crises around the world for 30 years. There are, sadly, many similarities between the situation in Puerto Rico and some of the difficult situations we have experienced elsewhere in the world. But one feature that is absolutely unique is that this is 3.5 million American citizens and they can leave Puerto Rico and move to the 50 states, and they will leave Puerto Rico and move to the 50 states in increasing numbers unless and until the situation is dealt with.

So your tax base, as was just mentioned, is going to walk out the door. And if there is an excessive imposition of austerity, well, there is a much better deal waiting for these American citizens in Florida, or Texas, or Pennsylvania, including access to the minimum-wage laws, including access to the earned-income tax credit, including access to fully funded or better-funded Medicare and Medicaid.

The second point I would like to make is with regard to the oversight board. I think that part of the bill is very good, Mr. Bishop. I think, to Mr. Pierluisi's question, which is directly at the point, you have worked very hard and, I think, found a balance between effective oversight and maintaining sufficient sovereignty for the elected officials, the Governor, and the legislature of Puerto Rico.

I do have one reservation or concern, if I may express it. I know that there are a lot of compromises already that have been made, but you did make reference, Mr. Chairman, to U.S. precedents for this kind of situation. I thought that in the case of the District of Columbia, the control board members had been selected by the President of the United States in consultation with the leadership of the relevant committees. The structure that you have is a different one, and I worry about the potential for difficulties in appointment, for deadlock in decisionmaking, and, of course, for some difficult moments with regard to the venue of jurisdiction and, as Mr. Weiss said, some key moments in the restructuring process.

My third point is about the restructuring authority. And here, I am afraid—well, I am not afraid—I completely agree with Mr. Weiss and the Treasury Department, I think that this is not yet a sufficiently streamlined process. I think, as I think most of the panel would agree, that you want a process which encourages voluntary renegotiation. It also prevents holdouts, a significant number of creditors refusing to negotiate in good faith.

And those safeguards for the majority of the creditors as well as for the people of Puerto Rico, those safeguards have to be present in the process it leads up to, a court-run adjudication, when the matter is before the courts themselves, and when the restructuring has ended, when you exit from what we are not calling bankruptcy, but what is obviously inspired by some of the better parts of U.S. bankruptcy process.

46

I understand very well that the House is also considering and thinking about financial distress and potential bankruptcy for systemically important financial institutions, a completely different matter. But the parallel, Mr. Chairman, is this: that I think the Republican caucus has rightly considered the importance of making sure that everyone, every individual, every company, and every legal entity in the United States can go bankrupt or can go through the equivalent of a bankruptcy process with appropriate safeguards, with protections for creditors, and recognizing the traditions of the United States, but also not allowing deadlock, impasse, and debt restructuring to get stuck.

So, I really encourage you to work further on Title III and the subsequent titles to move that restructuring authority in that direction. I am confident, Mr. Bishop, that you can and will ultimately get to a good bill.

Thank you.

[The prepared statement of Dr. Johnson follows:]

PREPARED STATEMENT OF SIMON JOHNSON, RONALD KURTZ PROFESSOR OF ENTREPRENEURSHIP, MIT SLOAN SCHOOL OF MANAGEMENT; SENIOR FELLOW, PETERSON INSTITUTE FOR INTERNATIONAL ECONOMICS; AND CO-FOUNDER OF HTTP:// BASELINESCENARIO.COM [1]

A. OVERVIEW

1. Puerto Rico is in the midst of a serious crisis. The economy is in decline, public health is threatened, and residents are moving to the 50 states. Unless there is a significant improvement in living conditions and job prospects, out-migration will likely pick up speed in the months and years ahead.

2. Making promised debt payments has—as a result of much broader stress on public finances—become difficult and, by some measures, Puerto Rico is already in default.

3. As a territory of the United States, Puerto Rico does not have access to the standard debt restructuring mechanisms available to the 50 states.

4. Compared with the situation for states and municipal borrowers within states, the U.S. Congress has much broader ultimate authority over all aspects of public finance in Puerto Rico. Some powers can be, have been, and should be delegated to Puerto Rico. But Congress must now decide on what broad strategy is adopted for dealing with the crisis in Puerto Rico.

5. Insisting on full repayment of all debts would be counterproductive. Most residents of Puerto Rico are also U.S. citizens. By moving to the 50 states, these people automatically can participate fully in more vibrant economies, while also changing their relationship to public finances—specifically, becoming eligible for the earned income tax credit.

6. It is no surprise that current net out-migration is around 60,000 per year and the population has declined by nearly 500,000 over 15 years.

7. Attempting to repay all of Puerto Rico's debts would involve either large further tax increases or significant cuts in public services or both. Either way, the incentive to leave the island will be stronger—and the tax base (people who earn income) will literally fly away. The odds of full repayment in that scenario are almost zero. And the social costs—in terms of lower living standards for those who remain—would be dramatic.

[1] Also a member of the Federal Deposit Insurance Corporation's Systemic Resolution Advisory Committee, the Office of Financial Research's Financial Research Advisory Committee, and the independent Systemic Risk Council (created by Sheila Bair). All the views expressed here are mine alone. An electronic version of this document can be found at http://BaselineScenario.com. For important disclosures, see http://baselinescenario.com/about/.

8. The best way forward includes agreeing on a mechanism for restructuring Puerto Rico's debts, with the goal of making a voluntary negotiation easier and more effective. The restructured debt should include some standard debt commitments, but with lower principal as well as reduced cash-flow commitment in the near term. At the same time, it would be very helpful if creditors could be persuaded to accept bonds with a contingent payoff—so that lenders get paid more if the economy does better.

9. At the same time, it is necessary to change the organization of public finance in Puerto Rico. The ability of the governor and the legislature to do this by themselves has proven to be limited. Establishing an oversight board would help build credibility.

10. At the same time, long experience—including with International Monetary Fund program lending—suggests that imposing institutional arrangements or even specific polices on countries does not usually lead to good outcomes.

11. The proposed legislation has some strong points in terms of creating an oversight board that would bring meaningful changes to governance, without being overly intrusive. However, I am concerned that the way in which board members are picked may slow the debt restructuring process. More on this is in Section B below.

12. In terms of the debt restructuring mechanism, the current draft of the bill is a great improvement over previous versions. However, there are a number of significant dimensions that require further clarification—including the extent to which debt principal can be reduced, whether all debt issued by Puerto Rico government entities can be readily included in any restructuring, and the mechanism through which a debt restructuring agreement is concluded. I expand on these points in Section C.

13. In addition, I am concerned about opening the door to reducing the minimum wage in Puerto Rico. Again, it is not in the interest of creditors to encourage taxpayers to leave the island.

B. OVERSIGHT BOARD

The proposed legislation does a good job of balancing the need for greater oversight for public finance in Puerto Rico along with the important priority of maintaining sovereignty.

We should keep in mind one very important lesson from economic and political history—an oversight board that is too strong would be counterproductive. Unless there is sufficient local ownership of any reform program, that program fails to deliver sustained growth (and better outcomes for creditors).

There are seven main elements in the proposed structure under discussion today:

- The proposed law specifies what must be in the 5-year fiscal plan.
- This plan is approved by the oversight board (or not).
- The governor draws up this plan and can adjust it in the process of discussion with the board.
- The governor is also responsible for the annual budget.
- This budget can be revised by the legislature, as long as it remains consistent with the 5-year fiscal plan.
- The board watches out for variances from the fiscal plan and makes recommendations for course corrections.
- If the government fails to correct these variances, after repeated opportunities have been missed, then the board can do more.

It is important to note that in the current draft, the board cannot issue regulations or other rules over the objection of the government of Puerto Rico.

The board will terminate after 4 years of balanced budgets. This seems entirely appropriate—and consistent with what was required for the District of Columbia.

There are also strong ethics and conflict of interest rules for the oversight board. These are important both in terms of perceived legitimacy and to ensure the board remains effective throughout its duration.

However, I am concerned with how members of the oversight board would be selected. In the case of DC, board members were picked by the President, in consultation with the leadership of the relevant congressional committees. In the current draft for Puerto Rico, the structure is more cumbersome and perhaps would lead to unintended outcomes.

For example, if the Speaker of the House proposed a list with only two names on it, would the President have to accept those names—or could he (or she) request a new list? How long would this process take?

C. DEBT RESTRUCTURING

With regard to the ability of the government of Puerto Rico to restructure its debts, I understand these provisions were controversial and the subject of much discussion. I also recognize that key details in this draft may shift as the legislation moves through Congress, so let me emphasize that the points made here apply to this particular wording—and even minor shifts in language could be sufficient reason to change my opinion.

Title III represents a great improvement over previous attempts to address the restructuring issue. However, the current language (also in Title VI) suggests that the process could be streamlined further in ways that would be helpful.

In particular, I would flag four issues which, at the very least, would benefit from greater clarity.

First, any and all forms of Puerto Rico official sector debt should be eligible for a reduction in principal as a result of the debt restructuring process. The bill's language could usefully be clarified in this regard.

Second, it should not be possible for creditors to prevent or delay a particular class of debt from being restructured. The current draft seems to create the possibility of a very slow process, for example for COFINA bonds.

Third, there needs to be a clear and workable mechanism through which a debt restructuring is concluded. At present there may be potential for relatively few creditors to delay or even prevent a final agreement. It is important not to allow any kind of hold out in this situation.

Fourth, while the goal is a voluntary comprehensive renegotiation of Puerto Rico's debt, the legislation could also recognize more explicitly that—under some circumstances—it may be necessary for a judge to impose a deal.

———

The CHAIRMAN. Thank you. We appreciate that.

We will now turn to our committee. Under Rule 3(d), questions are limited to 5 minutes for members of the committee. We will now recognize members for the questions they wish to ask.

Mr. Lamborn, are you ready to go first?

Mr. LAMBORN. Certainly, Mr. Chairman. And I want to thank the staff and you, Mr. Chairman. No one has worked harder on this than you have.

And I am still gathering information about this very complicated issue. I am looking with an open mind at the bill. I have questions and concerns though, and I hope that my questions will clarify, at least for me, some of what these are.

Thank you all for being here today.

We are all concerned about the future of Puerto Rico. We want it to be a successful, thriving economy. We want this crisis to end, and end in such a way where it will not happen again. And we want everyone to be treated fairly—creditors, pensioners, everyday citizens, and so on.

I am going to ask a question about the oversight board. I will use that phrase because that is what the bill calls it. The oversight board—I am a little unclear as to whether or not it has the final say in what a plan is that it thinks is necessary to get out of the crisis for the future. And I see some conflicting things in the bill.

So if someone could sort of distill for me the essence of what the power of the oversight board is. Is it really something that is going to make a difference, or will it be over-ridden if the Governor or legislature do not like its recommendations? To me, this is a critical issue.

Who would like to take a crack at that?

Mr. WEISS. I can start. Thank you, Congressman.

The oversight board does respect, in fact, the principles that the Administration laid out at the beginning of this process, which is that it preserves the Commonwealth's self-governance, while putting in place safeguards that ensure that the plans that are agreed and that the budgets that are agreed will be carried out.

And I think as other witnesses have testified, it is also the case uniquely in this bill that access to restructuring authorities or, indeed, access to a collective-action clause under the voluntary path can only be obtained through a process which is certified and put forward by the oversight board.

So, the oversight board respects the self-governance but is a gateway to further the voluntary negotiations that have a chance of success or restructuring authorities.

Mr. LAMBORN. What if the board and the Governor and/or legislature are at loggerheads on what the way forward is on an important part of the economy of Puerto Rico?

Mr. WEISS. The Governor and the legislature are to put forward a long-term fiscal plan and an annual budget. These are to be approved by the legislature, as is the case presently. In the event that subsequent budgets deviate from the initial fiscal plan, which is revised annually as well, or performance falls short, there is an iterative process back and forth with the oversight board to correct those shortfalls, and, ultimately, there is assurance that the plans will be carried out as initially forecast.

Mr. LAMBORN. OK. Thank you very much. That, to me, is critical.

Another critical item—there are so many here, but in my remaining short time—is the rights of creditors who feel like they are not getting a good deal, the holdout creditors, let's say.

And, sir, you have been intimately involved with this in the past. What about holdout creditors, even if they are in the minority, how will they be treated?

Mr. KIRPALANI. Sure. Thank you, Congressman Lamborn.

There are two types of holdouts. And the first type to think about is the dissenting minority when the majority of a pool or a class wants to go along with the deal and get a voluntary restructuring. You may have people who just do not want to participate. They don't want to even open their mail. They don't want to be involved in any kind of restructuring discussion or they are not sophisticated or they don't want to hire professionals to focus on their rights. So they may vote against or they may not vote at all.

The bill allows in the debt-restructuring section that the majority—it is majority in number, so more than 50 percent in number of people voting—and more than two-thirds in dollar amount of the particular class voting should be able to bind everyone in that class of similarly situated creditors.

So, the most important thing to take away, you have to make sure the bill protects similarly situated creditors to work together and not lump people with different contract rights, different property rights together.

The one issue I have with collective-action clauses is——

The CHAIRMAN. You have 3 seconds to say your issue.

Mr. KIRPALANI [continuing]. It is a eurozone concept. It has no classification rules. Just be careful.

The CHAIRMAN. OK. Thank you.

Mr. LAMBORN. Thank you.

The CHAIRMAN. Mr. Grijalva.

Mr. GRIJALVA. Thank you, Mr. Chairman.

Mr. Weiss, we know who loses if something pragmatic and humanitarian is not done in terms of legislation from this Congress. We know who loses. But if something is not done, who wins?

Mr. WEISS. Congressman, my answer is simple: no one wins, everyone loses. The people of Puerto Rico lose. The creditors ultimately lose. As has been noted, the moratorium, which has been enacted in Puerto Rico to preserve essential services, has led credit prices to deteriorate. And the mainland loses, in the sense that the alternative to this legislation, which is not a bailout, will, in fact, become a bailout over time.

And, as has been stated by many Members of Congress in both parties, this legislation costs taxpayers nothing. In fact, what it does is it precludes the likelihood that over time taxpayers would have to step in, as they always do when the safety and economic prosperity of Americans are at stake.

Mr. GRIJALVA. Thank you.

Professor Johnson, categorize for me the level of austerity that has been imposed on the people of Puerto Rico, specifically how much money has been cut from annual spending since, let's say, 2006, 2008.

Dr. JOHNSON. I do not have that precise number, but it is a significant amount of austerity. This is not of the levels that we have seen in Greece, but it is certainly the level that we have seen, for example, in Portugal in the eurozone. So a 10- to 20-percent cut in effective social services.

And, of course, you see a lot of this in the availability of doctors who have left. You see it in the hospital services. You see it in the hospitals laying off. The length of lines have increased for these essential services. So, it is not all in the monetary numbers, Congressman, it is also in the quality of services and the availability of those services.

Mr. GRIJALVA. In rough-number estimations, if that is the range, 20 percent—I think Governor Padilla said that, as well, about $500 billion—if that is the range, how much of Puerto Rico debt do hedge funds own at this point?

Dr. JOHNSON. I think you should ask the creditors' representatives for more precise numbers on their existing holdings. I think Mr. Kirpalani said that the mutual funds are holding 50 percent now, or no more than 50 percent of the debt. Presumably some is held by individuals, but the hedge funds are a significant portion of the remainder.

Mr. GRIJALVA. Mr. Weiss, do you have an estimate on how much of that debt is hedge fund?

Mr. WEISS. I think estimates vary from a third on up.

I should mention that this debt continues to trade hands every day and is trading today, as well, and so this number, by most estimates, is accumulating.

Mr. GRIJALVA. Just to review, the point that I think is important to note is that if hedge funds bought risky Puerto Rican bonds as an investment strategy, they structure the investments to absorb a hit in the event some of those investments do not go well. They have spent heavily to prevent the debt from being restructured in the courts. They have spent heavily to try to prevent restructuring here in Congress. I think this is the kind of strategy that makes people really angry in Washington. And it is an investment strategy by the hedge funders in this particular instance.

Unfortunately, as I asked in the earlier question, nobody wins. It is at the expense of the quality of life for the people of Puerto Rico.

I think that somebody holding that significant number and being not only the holdouts but also effectively attempting to campaign against any movement on this issue legislatively, I think, speaks for itself in terms of what greed has caused in terms of us being able to find a solution to this.

With that, Mr. Chairman, I yield back.

The CHAIRMAN. Thank you.

Mr. Wittman.

Mr. WITTMAN. Thank you, Mr. Chairman.

I would like to thank the witnesses for joining us today.

Professor Kent, I want to start with you. You laid out the constitutional authorities—Article I, where Congress can act on the issues of bankruptcy; Article IV that empowers it to act on issues involving territories.

My question is this. As you look at other provisions there under Article III for the courts to adjudicate bankruptcies, do you believe that there is a priority that is set in the Constitution that says the Congress must act, and counter to the courts, where the courts could act to adjudicate a bankruptcy such as this?

Mr. KENT. Well, the power to adjudicate bankruptcy has to be given by the Congress, and the courts cannot act unless that authority is given. So a bill, such as the one being contemplated now by the committee, would be the first thing that would need to happen before we would have any questions about power of courts.

Mr. WITTMAN. But the courts could act, in this case, to adjudicate this?

Mr. KENT. Were they granted authority by the Congress, yes.

Mr. WITTMAN. But in absence of a congressional action, the courts can act to adjudicate this. The creditors can file and say, "we wish that our claims be made before the court," and they can argue their claims before the court.

Mr. KENT. I am not a bankruptcy law expert. I am a constitutional person, but my understanding is that, currently, Puerto Rico and its instrumentalities are not—that bankruptcy is not available to them through the current statute.

Mr. WITTMAN. Mr. Weiss, a question to you. When we talk about how this should be laid out and Congress acting versus what I believe can take place through the courts, why wouldn't it be a desire for voluntary agreements to be worked out between Puerto Rico, the bondholders, through a mechanism in the courts versus one that is set by Congress? And does Congress' action actually itself set priorities for creditors' claims versus where it could be worked out in the courts with voluntary agreements and back and forth between the judiciary and the government of Puerto Rico?

Mr. WEISS. Congressman, the litigation has already begun in courts. At the time that the Governor was forced to claw back certain revenues in order to pay other debts in December, there was immediate litigation filed.

Mr. WITTMAN. So there is current litigation? They are trying to adjudicate their claims?

Mr. WEISS. There is current litigation, and none of this is reaching resolution. It is not resulting in a constructive environment for negotiations to take place. To the contrary, as these claims are individually pursued, both against the Commonwealth and amongst the different creditors, there are 24 creditor classes and counting. What we fear is that if we are left without any framework, as has been established by the committee under leadership of the Chairman, that Puerto Rico faces a lost decade as these various claims are contested.

Mr. WITTMAN. Why would the contestment take place any differently with back and forth between the bondholders and the courts versus the government of Puerto Rico bondholders and the United States Congress?

Mr. WEISS. Two reasons. First, this legislation puts in place a strict and independent oversight board in order to look across all of the different claims and the fiscal plan and budgeting process and to try to bring all of that into alignment through the course of a restructuring.

And second, in the tools that have been outlined by the draft, there is an opportunity to pursue a voluntary pathway and to achieve agreement across a particular class of creditors as there is an opportunity to pursue an orderly restructuring mechanism in the event that the voluntary process fails.

Mr. WITTMAN. Does this potential legislation, though, reprioritize what would otherwise be the claims of the bondholders here? In other words, does Congress supersede or put its imprint over who it believes should take precedence in that versus an adjudicatory hearing where the courts would determine priority of the bondholders?

Mr. WEISS. There is language in the bill, which I will not cite exactly because it is relatively fresh, which does talk about the pre-existing priorities of claims, but what is to be pointed out is that without the centralized review of an oversight board and without the restructuring authorities and voluntary mechanism, there will be endless litigation as to claims.

We have heard from secured creditors on this panel. There are other creditors who are actually of a different point of view as to who is most senior, and so, in order to bring this to an orderly resolution, it requires this kind of mechanism. Without it, we fear economic chaos.

Mr. WITTMAN. Thank you, Mr. Chairman.

I yield back.

The CHAIRMAN. Thank you.

Ms. Bordallo.

Ms. BORDALLO. Thank you, Mr. Chairman. I truly appreciate your leadership and being true to your word to craft a bill to assist

Puerto Rico, and I, as a representative from a territory, am also very concerned.

I appreciate the language that clarifies the other territories covered by this provision must opt in to the control through a vote of the legislature and with concurrence of our governors. While I can empathize with the policy decision to try to keep the bill clean, unfortunately, the problems of this fiscal crisis are cross-jurisdictional. The debt crisis will not be resolved through debt restructuring alone but, rather, will need additional fixes.

Guam and the other territories, while we are nowhere near the crisis that Puerto Rico is in, could very well be headed down that road should these fixes not be addressed. So, thus, I remain disappointed that the bill does not address issues such as Medicaid, the EITC, and government pensions. I, and the other delegates from the territory, sent a letter to the committee last week reiterating our support for these fixes.

The Administration's proposal includes the other territories in removing the caps on the Medicaid program, readjusting our FMAPs, as well as providing a cover over to the nearer Tax Code jurisdiction on providing EITC.

I simply do not believe that the proposals that we are looking at now will resolve Puerto Rico's problems. So we are doing all that we can to be proactive in ensuring that what is happening to Puerto Rico does not happen to the rest of us.

So, Mr. Weiss, I have a question for you. This bill authorizes an oversight board and debt restructuring for Puerto Rico which will address their debt crisis. However, will this legislation fix their cash-flow issue or help with the other issues I have mentioned, such as Medicaid or EITC? Wouldn't it be helpful for this to be included and for the territories to be considered in this fix as well?

And, if you could make your answer brief, because I have very little time.

Mr. WEISS. Yes, our initial proposal did include those two components, as you are well aware. However, it does alleviate the financial stress on the Commonwealth through the stay and through the process, which would allow the Commonwealth to have a sustainable level of debt, which is our ultimate goal.

Ms. BORDALLO. Thank you very much.

Professor Johnson, you are an advocate for an investment-led recovery for Puerto Rico, and I understand that you have also cautioned that reducing the minimum wage would induce more Puerto Ricans to leave. So I ask: Does keeping the minimum wage at $4.25 an hour increase the likelihood of (1) more Puerto Ricans having to rely on government assistance and/or (2) more Puerto Ricans having to leave the island for better economic opportunity?

How would this minimum wage provision impact the long-term economic outlook for Puerto Rico?

Dr. JOHNSON. I believe the Governor would have to choose to opt in to this minimum wage provision, as I read the bill. If that were the case, then I would be very worried about the consequences, Congresswoman, for exactly the reasons that you just articulated.

Ms. BORDALLO. Thank you.

And, Mr. Weiss, I have my third question and last question. The bill clearly prohibits elected officials from Puerto Rico from serving on the control board. Now, I understand that, while not explicit, there is a conflict-of-interest provision that would also prevent representatives with ties to bondholders from serving. Is this provision sufficient to prevent any potential conflicts of interest?

Mr. WEISS. We continue to work with the committee to refine this provision. We agree with the principle that this committee should be fully independent of the political process and free of any conflict of interest, whether financial or otherwise.

Ms. BORDALLO. Thank you very much.

Mr. Chairman, I yield back.

The CHAIRMAN. Thank you.

Mr. Gohmert.

Mr. GOHMERT. Thank you, Mr. Chair.

I appreciate your testimony today.

I understood that, previously, there had been mention of a 10 to 20 percent cut in social programs being proposed in Puerto Rico, and I am curious: Does anybody know if there are proposals of cutting the government workers by 10 to 20 percent, or is it just social benefits? Anyone know?

Dr. JOHNSON. Well, we were discussing, Congressman, a moment ago the cuts that have already been made since 2006, so that was a retrospective assessment. And, of course, the government payroll has also been cut over that same period as part of that.

Mr. GOHMERT. This same cut, 10 to 20 percent?

Dr. JOHNSON. Again, I do not have those exact numbers with me, but we can look them up very easily.

Mr. GOHMERT. Yes.

Dr. JOHNSON. It is certainly above 10 percent. One of the concerns is the way in which those layoffs have impacted services, who has been laid off, and so on. But, again, that is a retrospective statement.

Mr. GOHMERT. I have seen one projection that 20 percent of all income in Puerto Rico came from Federal welfare benefits from those paying Federal taxes in the 50 states and, unfortunately, for the District of Columbia, for DC, too, so I am curious, of the reforms that you refer to as retrospective, that were 10 to 20 percent of social benefit cuts, were those cuts that Puerto Rico is making to Puerto Ricans, because my understanding is that it certainly was not cuts to social benefits from the Federal Treasury?

Dr. JOHNSON. No. I think what we were discussing, because of the nature of fiscal autonomy in Puerto Rico, is they have a different basis for their revenue. There are people who receive Medicare benefits and the people who pay into and receive Social Security.

Mr. GOHMERT. Right.

Dr. JOHNSON. But they are not paying favorable income tax, as you know, and it is the collapse in local revenue, including the sales tax, that has had a significant impact on revenue.

Mr. GOHMERT. One of the remarkable things, Puerto Rico ought to be the model for how free markets could work. It could be the United States' Hong Kong, because there is no Federal income tax. All it would need is to streamline and not have such a bloated government where, I have seen the numbers—one community of 1,800 or so, 45-plus percent work for the government, and then the list goes on down. A community of 35,000, 40 percent of those work for the government. Another community, 27,000, 39 percent work for the government.

If it were not for all the government workers in Puerto Rico, there would be no need to have a 4-percent higher corporate tax than the United States itself has. We have the highest corporate tax of any advanced nation in the world, 35 percent. Yet, Puerto Rico has more than that at 39 percent. I would think that with no Federal income tax, if you get it down to around 12 percent, business would be flocking, but nobody wants to come to a place where 45 percent of the community works for the government. That does not wreak of free markets, growing businesses.

And then it seems one of the real tragedies—on the one hand, we are told if we will allow an exception for Puerto Rico to lower the minimum wage, then that will create more jobs and that will get more Puerto Ricans working, because we did provide an exception when the Democrats had the majority for one of our territories, but that was not Puerto Rico.

But then when I see a projection that a family of three, the take-home pay for doing a minimum wage job at the current level would be less than $1,200, but with the U.S. Federal welfare, AFDC welfare, food stamps, the take-home is more like $1,800. Then if we lower the minimum wage, then there is even less take-home for those who might be tempted to work for about two-thirds of what they get if they do not work.

My time is expiring, but I would welcome anything in writing from any of our witnesses that would tell us how to balance that problem. Thank you.

I yield back.

The CHAIRMAN. OK. You have your assignment.

Ms. Tsongas.

Mr. TSONGAS. Thank you, Mr. Chairman.

And I appreciate all of you being here with us today. As we are talking about Puerto Rico, I just want to reiterate the way in which it makes it back to our districts.

The economic viability and success of Puerto Rico is an issue that is really important to many of my constituents in my district in Massachusetts. One in five of my constituents identify as Hispanic or Latino, and 40 percent of them are from Puerto Rico. So many of them have friends and family who still live there. They have seen firsthand the devastating effects that the 10-year recession and debt crisis have had on the island, and they are watching carefully as we work to address it. They are well aware of what the 3.5 million American citizens are struggling with.

Puerto Rico's electricity prices are higher than any state in the country. The unemployment rate is 12.2 percent, more than double that across the United States, and its poverty rate is a staggering 45 percent. And we are hearing today about the alarming decline in some essential services.

We, in Congress, have a responsibility to address the crisis facing Puerto Rico, and I think the discussion draft and the bipartisan effort behind it is a step toward that goal. All stakeholders stand to lose in the face of the continued deterioration on the island is its economic and financial condition.

I appreciate the debate we are having about the different elements of the legislation, but as the Ranking Member of the Federal Lands Subcommittee, a committee that is tasked with the protection of our shared historical, cultural, and national heritage, I just want to express my deep concern about the bill's provision to transfer public land at the Vieques National Wildlife Refuge. This refuge is one of the crown jewels of our National Wildlife Refuge System, and the transfer language is an unnecessary addition that will do absolutely nothing to address the fiscal crisis in Puerto Rico.

With that, I would like to yield the balance of my time to Mr. Pierluisi.

Mr. PIERLUISI. Thank you, Ms. Tsongas.

Actually, I will use this time to clarify a couple of points, and the witnesses can correct me if I am wrong.

Mr. Lamborn, the way the bill currently reads, the Federal oversight board does have the power to approve the fiscal plan of the government of Puerto Rico. It also has the power to approve the budgets, approved in turn by the legislature and signed by the Governor, so the board does have ultimate authority.

The bill defers to the government of Puerto Rico in the right way because it allows the Governor to elaborate the plan and submit it to the board, and the board can bring it back and send it back with its comments and recommendations. So, it will be a back and forth until the board is satisfied that the fiscal plan makes sense. OK.

On the budgets, the process is similar. The Governor will submit the budget to the board for review. The board will comment. Once the board blesses the budget at that level, then it goes to the legislature of Puerto Rico. The legislature will do its job. But before it is finally approved by the legislature, the board will take a look at it, and the board can say that the board is not satisfied with the budget as approved by the legislature. So, the board will have the final say in a way.

What I expect to happen here is—just assume that the Governor and the legislature of Puerto Rico will do the right thing. They will just have this board overseeing them in this process. The same applies on variances. Let's assume that there is overspending, meaning that the spending is excessive, given the budget that is applied. What the legislation does, it requires quarterly reports to the board, and the board can say, when they see overspending: Explain to us the variance. And if the explanation is reasonable, nothing happens. If, after multiple tries, the government of Puerto Rico cannot satisfy the board's concerns, then the board can step in.

So that is why this is a reasonable model, given that you do have elected officials in Puerto Rico, a Governor and legislators, so it does give the board the final say.

On the minimum wage, let me say this. The way the bill is drafted, the Governor of Puerto Rico is the one that can opt to pay less than the minimum wage to employees 25 years or younger. I personally do not like that bill provision, and I will tell you why: it will promote migration out of Puerto Rico, because these are U.S. citizens, and if not, they will not work, and they will simply rely on welfare and the informal economy.

The CHAIRMAN. Thank you.

Mr. Fleming.

Dr. FLEMING. Thank you, Mr. Chairman.

Mr. Weiss, does this legislation contain mandatory debt restructuring ability for the control board?

Mr. WEISS. At the end of the process, this ensures that the debts will be restructured to a level that is sustainable relative to the size of the economist——

Dr. FLEMING. So the answer is yes.

Mr. WEISS. At the end of the process.

Dr. FLEMING. OK. So what this does is create a control board, which then goes to the creditors and asks them to come up with or to go along with some sort of voluntary negotiated prioritization of the creditors. If they disagree, then you go to the next step, the step you are referring to, which some call a cramdown, where then they will be forced to restructure. Am I correct on that?

Mr. WEISS. It organizes both the voluntary discussion, which you are describing, and the restructuring mechanism in the event that the voluntary restructuring does not succeed. It also incentivizes the voluntary restructuring with tools which are not in place today.

Dr. FLEMING. So the answer is yes, it does have the power to force restructuring.

So does that mean that it is possible for holders of full faith and credit debt to be put at a lower priority for repayment than unions or pensions?

Mr. WEISS. We are not here to pick winners and losers among creditors.

Dr. FLEMING. But that can happen. Is that correct?

Mr. WEISS. The oversight board is invested with enormous responsibility in putting forth, as the Congressman has described.

Dr. FLEMING. But don't dodge the question. Can that happen?

Mr. WEISS. It can only happen if all other measures have been exhausted and it is the judgment of the oversight group——

Dr. FLEMING. But it can happen, correct?

Mr. WEISS. These creditors today are holding 67 cents on the dollar. They know it is being restructured, sir.

Dr. FLEMING. Let me ask you this. They say that this is not bankruptcy or reorganization bankruptcy, but it looks like reorganization bankruptcy, so how is this, other than just the technical features of it, overall, how is it different than a bankruptcy?

Mr. WEISS. It is radically different from bankruptcy.

Dr. FLEMING. Let me hear from you.

Mr. KIRPALANI. Yes, I would just like to try to answer the Congressman's very important question. The way this bill is drafted, it protects priorities. It does not disturb local law. We could tighten that. In fact, our view is it should be tightened.

Dr. FLEMING. But, in a sense, that bankruptcy could force, cramdown, if you will, require a certain priority of creditors, isn't that also true of this bill as well?

Mr. KIRPALANI. Only if the dissenting class has no good reason to hold up because they are getting the best interest, the same that we get under law——

Dr. FLEMING. In other words, if they do not agree, this control board can force them to reprioritize, correct?

Mr. KIRPALANI. No. They would have their ability to explain to the court, to your colleagues on your left, that this is an unfair plan; it discriminates unfairly to me. The laws can be drafted even more tightly and clearly, and we would support that, but if the intent of the bill is absolutely to protect the——

Dr. FLEMING. If the board did not agree with them, then they would be forced.

Mr. KIRPALANI. But that is no different than in the absence of legislation.

Dr. FLEMING. Again, that looks a lot like bankruptcy restructuring, so I would just have to say—now, it is also said that this is not a bailout.

But we understand, now, how did we get here to begin with? It is the progressive socialist policies, economic policies that got Puerto Rico at this point, the same kind of policies that got Greece where it is today. Greece has gone through two restructurings with bailouts, as I recall, and they are going to have to go through another one.

From my perspective, I look at this, and I am told: this is no bailout. Well, technically, that is true, but there are still going to be cash-flow problems. How are we going to solve the cash-flow problems?

Mr. KIRPALANI. I think that there are a lot of things that Congress can do under the territories clause to create better growth, better initiatives. What this is doing, it is the first step; it is a necessary step to stabilize the economy to keep people in place.

Dr. FLEMING. Exactly, that is my point. It is the first step, and what is the next step? What is the other shoe to drop?

Mr. KIRPALANI. I don't know that there will be.

Dr. FLEMING. There will have to be a cash bailout. That is the only way that is going to be solved under this bill.

Mr. KIRPALANI. Without this bill, there will be a cash bailout.

Dr. FLEMING. I would suggest to you that this is a framework of a bankruptcy, whatever you want to call it, and it will ultimately require a bailout.

I yield back.

Mr. KIRPALANI. But it will respect priorities, though.

The CHAIRMAN. Mr. Pierluisi.

Mr. PIERLUISI. Thank you, Chairman.

Mr. Weiss, I would like you to expand, elaborate on your concerns with the collective action clause, the way it is currently drafted. As I understand it, your concern is that it is too cumbersome, or it is not streamlined enough. You want this to work, but can you expand? What is wrong with the collective action clause process that this bill provides for?

Mr. WEISS. Congressman, we believe that the intent is for this to work, that there are important drafting items which we need to review with the committee, and we will begin to do so immediately following this hearing, but the intent is to provide for a voluntary path with incentives to reach agreement and, in the event that this fails, a restructuring mechanism to allow the Commonwealth to emerge with a sustainable debt load.

If these principles are respected in the drafting, we believe we can work with the committee to get there.

Mr. PIERLUISI. OK. Now, Mr. Miller, as I understood your testimony, you are saying that, in general terms, the markets are welcoming this bill. The markets are looking forward to a restructuring, and in your view, it is better to have an orderly restructuring process as opposed to litigation all over the place. That is how I read what you said.

As I see it, when we talk about collective action clause—these terms get in the way, but let me explain them, and then you correct me—and cramdown, what we are talking about is, any time you want to restructure debt, you want to reach all the creditors of the entity in question. If you don't reach them all, then the deal will mean so much, and when you need to restructure, again, you try to reach them all.

So collective action is another way of saying: If you have two-thirds majority of the creditors supporting the deal, then you can go to court to enforce the deal on all, and the same pretty much applies on the cramdown concept.

What is happening in Puerto Rico is that we can negotiate with the creditors of PREPA, the power company, and we can negotiate with the creditors of the water and sewer company, but we cannot reach them all. We do not have a structure.

Would you comment, Mr. Miller?

Mr. MILLER. Sure. Thank you very much for the question, Congressman. The reasons why I did allude to the fact that I think the marketplace is prepared and more welcoming in this bill is for the following reasons: The independence of the board, getting fresh audits, getting transparency over what the fiscal situation actually is; those are all positives to the marketplace, as a whole. The determination of the level of debt that the Commonwealth of Puerto Rico can actually handle longer term and grow the economy and be a stable credit, that is positive.

I think versus alternatives—the litigation is building, the defaults are coming regardless, and I think the marketplace, you can see in the pricing, the marketplace knows that is going to happen anyway. The 67 percent figure that you are alluding to, that is, in part, this is a large and very diverse widely held set of bonds and set of indentures, and in such a circumstance, you will never get to 100 percent. It is impossible.

Mr. PIERLUISI. Thank you. Let me quickly address you, Mr. Kirpalani, and the audience. This is not Chapter 9. I have a Chapter 9 bill. Mr. Duffy had a Chapter 9 bill. This is not super Chapter 9. Why not? Because there is a Federal oversight board acting as the gatekeeper here, making sure there is no abuse of the Chapter 9 process, of the bankruptcy rules.

There is nothing wrong with the bankruptcy rules. Congress enacted them, but we want them to be applied fairly, and that is why you have this board being created to oversee this. Do you agree, Mr. Kirpalani?

Mr. KIRPALANI. Thank you, Congressman.

I 100 percent agree with that statement, and I would also say that our laws, our bankruptcy laws and restructuring laws from 100 years, they are the envy of the world. They are the hallmark of an efficient financial system, and I was hired several years ago by Dubai to pass legislation and help them draft it. They never even had to use it because every creditor organized itself and voluntarily agreed because they understood the rules, and the same thing can happen for Puerto Rico.

Mr. PIERLUISI. Thank you.

The CHAIRMAN. Thank you.

Mr. McClintock.

Mr. McCLINTOCK. Thank you, Mr. Chairman.

First of all, let me ask the question. Does Congress have the authority to change bankruptcy law or to take portions of bankruptcy law and apply it in this case?

Mr. KENT. Yes, it does. Under the territories clause, I believe it does.

Mr. McCLINTOCK. OK. And does it also have the authority to alter bankruptcy law as it applies to states?

Mr. KENT. As it applies to state governments?

Mr. McCLINTOCK. Yes.

Mr. KENT. That raises some very hard issues. The Supreme Court addressed this in the 1930s and had very serious constitutional concerns about the impact on state sovereignty. I would say pretty definitively that something like the oversight board that is contemplated here as kind of the quid pro quo for having access to restructuring would be——

Mr. McCLINTOCK. But the oversight board, though, I think is irrelevant to the principal point that we are altering the laws under which these loans were made to creditors. We are rewriting these laws for Puerto Rico, and if it can rewrite these laws for Puerto Rico, the concern arises, why wouldn't it then also rewrite them for states?

My concern is that every lender to every state in this country is no longer going to trust the terms of their own loans, and if those terms are not stable and reliable, interest rates will rise for every state in this country, and taxpayers are going to end up shouldering that burden through paying much higher interest costs. These are the concerns that are being expressed by a number of state governors with respect to the ramifications of this bill.

The argument I hear is: this is apples and oranges. Puerto Rico is a territory subject to congressional oversight, and states are not.

But the applicability of bankruptcy law can affect states, and Congress can rewrite bankruptcy law, whether for territories or for states, and this introduces a very, very dangerous precedent into a public borrowing.

It seems to me that, under the status quo, both sides have an incentive to negotiate mutually agreeable terms. If we were to simply honor the rule of law and maintain the terms in which these loans were originally made, first, I think it would be a very powerful signal to bond markets that the United States stands by its promises, even when it is inconvenient. Until the prospect of this congressional action arose, my understanding is Puerto Rico was negotiating terms of debt restructuring with the mutual consent of their creditors, and under current law, it is in the interest of both sides, the debtor and the creditor, to work out the terms with which both can live to restructure and repay this debt.

And I think it is also within the interests of the people of Puerto Rico to hold accountable the elected officials that got them into this mess, not an unelected and unaccountable oversight board.

Mr. WEISS. Congressman, with respect to the constitutionality, there is a clear pathway under Article IV of the Constitution for this to be enacted for territories. The 10th Amendment provides no such assurance.

Current negotiations, in our judgment, cannot succeed without the additional tools which have been effectively offered by this committee to support both voluntary negotiations and restructuring, if it is needed. The witness from Nuveen could speak to the efficacy of this with respect to state borrowing costs, but the pathway is between a disorderly default and something structured.

Mr. MCCLINTOCK. My time is very limited. I think the structure on that oversight board, it seems to me that it violates, indeed it renounces the most basic architecture of American constitutional government where the Founders meticulously divided and separated the powers of government. This board recombines them. And where the American Founders meticulously established a system where their government was accountable and with the consent of the people, this establishes an oversight board that is not accountable to the people of Puerto Rico.

And I think the great tragedy is this: Puerto Rico is an island paradise. It is a cruise ship destination. It is ideally located for both North and South Atlantic shipping. It has an ideal climate for agriculture. It is part of the United States. It has all of the protections of property rights and the rule of law and due process. The only thing that it lacks is wise public policy.

It seems to me that the direction we should be taking is relieving Puerto Rico of the burdens of the Jones Act, a panoply of regulatory burdens that are crushing the economy and providing the option for Puerto Rican companies to be taxed territorially. These reforms could turn Puerto Rico into the Hong Kong of the Caribbean, and that is the direction we ought to be taking: maintain the rule of law and restore free markets to Puerto Rico.

The CHAIRMAN. Mrs. Torres, you are next.

Mrs. TORRES. Thank you, Mr. Chairman. Good morning. My questions are around the board, and in the specific bill, I think that we are pretty prescriptive as to who appoints the seven-member board. However, it lacks the same type of prescriptive way of who actually can be appointed.

While the bill states that individuals must have knowledge and expertise in finance, municipal bond markets, management, law, or organization, or operation of business or government, seven board members could come from any one of those subgroups, but not all, correct?

Mr. Weiss, I apologize if I put you on the spot there.

Mr. WEISS. Not at all, I think that this is an area we continue to develop with the committee. I think that the principles for the composition have been established that it must be a deeply experienced board, an independent board, free of all conflict of interest and broadly representative of the stakeholders who are affected by the restructuring.

Mrs. TORRES. I understand the conflict of interest. However, my concern is still that all seven members could come from any one of those specific backgrounds, and I think that the board should be a diverse board that represents the interests that are being proposed here or talked about here, not just with financial interest but also that look like the people of Puerto Rico.

Mr. WEISS. We agree with you.

Mrs. TORRES. In the early 1980s, as a young 16-year-old, I started my first job earning minimum wage. Back then, it was $3.35. Fast forward 35 years, we are asking 25-year-olds and under in Puerto Rico to live within about 90 cents higher than the minimum wage of early 1980s. How is that not going to negatively impact the workforce of Puerto Rico? And is this going to create a two-class type of employee where the older employees may be the first ones to be laid off or fired under this restructuring of wages?

Mr. WEISS. Professor Johnson addressed this issue before eloquently. The perhaps single biggest crisis in Puerto Rico is out-migration. In the 12 months ending October 31, 2.5 percent of Puerto Ricans left for the mainland. That is roughly double the rate that were leaving 2 years ago, and this is why the comparison between Puerto Rico and Greece breaks—we are talking about Americans.

And it is true that Puerto Rico can be an island paradise. It is not a paradise for the American citizens who live there today. There is 58 percent childhood poverty; 45 percent of homes live in poverty. Government payrolls have been shrunk by more than 25 percent, and the policy of austerity, coupled with the suffocating amount of debt, has left the economy at a dead end. These are the tools which will allow Puerto Rico to emerge—and I repeat—at no cost to the Federal taxpayer.

Mrs. TORRES. These are the two issues that I am very concerned about, and I don't believe that today I have heard an answer that has satisfied my concern.

Thank you, and I yield back my time.

The CHAIRMAN. Mr. Benishek.

Dr. BENISHEK. Thank you, Mr. Chairman.

Thank you all for being here today. I am learning a lot. I guess I have a couple of basic questions here, and that is, what if we don't do anything, what is going to happen? Maybe, Mr. Kirpalani, you have some experience.

Mr. KIRPALANI. Thank you, Congressman Benishek. Yes, and we have seen what happens. If Congress does not do anything, then the local legislature does, in the cover of night, pass a debt moratorium law that denies due process and contravenes U.S. law. I think that is going to be met with constitutional challenges.

I am not blaming local legislators from doing what they need to do to protect the citizens living in their home jurisdiction, but it certainly does not uphold the rule of law. This Congress can do that, and so we hope that you do.

Dr. BENISHEK. Mr. Miller, what is going to happen to the bond markets, not only for Puerto Rico but around the country in general, if nothing happens here? What is the story with that?

Mr. MILLER. We think that Puerto Rican bonds generally have been moving more into distressed territory and investors have re-allocated, generally. That does not mean there could not be further downside. I think there is more collateral damage potentially on Puerto Rican security specifically in the absence of congressional action, and possibly some additional damage on the municipal bond market. Although, again, I would emphasize that this has moved heavily into distressed debt territory and therefore has moved heavily into hedge fund territory, and individual investors and mutual funds have dramatically reduced their exposure, and the municipal bond market is relatively healthy.

I would add that state borrowing costs actually continue to fall, and the risk premium on state borrowing costs above a pure AAA, those risk premiums have continued to narrow, meaning people are comfortable that states do not want Chapter 9. I know of no state that wants to go into Chapter 9, that needs to go into Chapter 9, or that would want a control board.

So, I think that I would continue to highlight the territorial specific nature, not just from a legal perspective, which is true, but also from the perspective that no state is in the same fiscal and economic situation that Puerto Rico is in. So, there are some very significant differences.

Dr. BENISHEK. Thank you.

I don't know who can answer this question, but I have some of the same concerns that Dr. Fleming had. If we do this, how is this going to fix all these problems? How is this going to fix the immediate cash-flow difficulties?

Mr. Weiss, can you comment on that?

Mr. WEISS. This, in our judgment, properly completed, will stabilize the crisis. The stay, coupled with the tools to incentivize voluntary negotiations and the restructuring mechanism, backed by an independent and strong fiscal oversight board, in our judgment, will create a period of stability, but we do agree that there needs to be additional tools over the long run to incentivize growth. Those do not need to come necessarily in the form——

Dr. BENISHEK. Well, give me an example of that.

Mr. WEISS. Our initial plan pointed to two. We believe in the earned income tax credit as a very effective way of—a bipartisan way of incentivizing work, bringing more Americans in Puerto Rico into the formal workforce, which has a tendency to expand the taxable base, and it also puts money into the pocket of those most likely to spend it.

Dr. BENISHEK. I appreciate that answer. I have heard in previous hearings about the potential for privatizing much of the industry that is currently owned by the government. But, how is this board going to make that happen or facilitate something happening that they change the way they do business there?

Mr. WEISS. In our discussions with business, it is clear that there is significant appetite to invest in Puerto Rico, both to modernize the electricity grid, to provide alternative forms of power generation, to invest in infrastructure. No one will invest in the face of an economic crisis. The crisis needs to be stabilized, and then the significant interest in investing in Puerto Rico will materialize.

Dr. BENISHEK. What kind of a timeline are we talking about for all this to happen? Say this bill passed tomorrow through the House and all that, what is the timeline you are talking about?

Mr. WEISS. For it to be done responsibly, for there to be an ample opportunity for creditors to negotiate in the voluntary process in order for the oversight board to implement its work in a thoughtful way and to provide the transparency of financials that we all seek, it will not happen overnight.

Dr. BENISHEK. You are wasting time here because my time is up now. I did not get an answer to my question.

Thank you, Mr. Chairman.

The CHAIRMAN. Just tell him "now." Just say "now."

Mr. WEISS. A year and a half, 2 years.

The CHAIRMAN. All right, Mr. Cartwright, you are recognized.

Mr. CARTWRIGHT. Thank you, Mr. Chairman.

And thank you to our witnesses for coming today to discuss a crisis that will shape Puerto Rico for decades to come and could have ripple effects across our entire Nation.

We all know the situation in Puerto Rico is dire. Congress has to act quickly to address this growing humanitarian crisis, but I do have grave concerns that some of the proposals concerning this crisis either have little to do with addressing the actual issue at hand or potentially could exacerbate problems for Puerto Rico in the long run.

Under current Federal law, if an employee is less than 20 years old and is in his or her first 90 days of working with a particular employer, Federal minimum wage laws allow the employer to pay them a sub-minimum wage of $4.25 an hour, and the justification, of course, is that they are apprentices and they are learning the trade of the job.

The draft of the bill we are considering tomorrow changes that. It allows the Governor of Puerto Rico to lower the minimum wage in Puerto Rico to $4.25 for anybody who is under 25 and is in their first 5 years on the job, not just 90 days.

Yet, there are professions that require 5 years of on-the-job training, some medical professions, plumbers or electricians, for example, but workers in these industries are generally rewarded with much higher salaries than minimum wage after their training is complete to help justify lower salaries, which are generally well above $4.25 anyway, while training.

Professor Johnson, I want to ask you, do you know of any minimum wage jobs that require 5 years of on-the-job training?

Dr. JOHNSON. I cannot readily bring to mind any such jobs, Congressman.

Mr. CARTWRIGHT. Me neither.

How about you, Mr. Weiss? Do you know of any such jobs, minimum wage jobs that require 5 years of on-the-job training?

Mr. WEISS. No, sir.

Mr. CARTWRIGHT. OK. Another issue I have a concern about is emigration. One of the drivers of the economic crisis in Puerto Rico is the roughly 100,000 people per year who are moving to the mainland for better economic opportunity. I am concerned that drastic measures, such the proposal surrounding minimum wage, could accelerate and exacerbate this emigration and deepen Puerto Rico's crisis in the long run.

According to the CDC, the average age for a new mom on the island is 24.1 years old, so a huge percentage of new moms in Puerto Rico would have to raise their child on potentially $4.25 an hour. I wouldn't stick around for that if I didn't have to.

Professor Johnson and Mr. Weiss, what does it mean for the economic recovery if young families leave the island?

Professor Johnson?

Dr. JOHNSON. That is your tax base walking out the door or getting on the plane and flying to the mainland. And the more people that leave, of course, Congressman, the more relatives you already have, the more connections you have, the easier it is to get a job, so it is a self-reinforcing process that is already accelerating, as you said and as Mr. Weiss has said.

Mr. CARTWRIGHT. And young families are crucial to anchoring the economic recovery, aren't they, Professor Johnson?

Dr. JOHNSON. Yes, of course. We need young people throughout the U.S. economy, including in Puerto Rico.

Mr. CARTWRIGHT. Do you agree with that?

Mr. WEISS. Fully agree.

Mr. CARTWRIGHT. OK.

Now, Professor Johnson, do you think at the end of 5 years of paying a worker a sub-minimum wage to the employee, companies will be more likely to value the training their employees will have accumulated and be happy then to pay the $7.25 an hour, or will this minimum wage provide an incentive to let these employees go and start a new clock with a new sub-minimum wage 20-year-old worker?

Dr. JOHNSON. I think that point was already made by Mrs. Torres. I think it is a very legitimate fear to consider, and I absolutely share it.

Mr. CARTWRIGHT. All right. So if that is the case and young workers put this together, they put two and two together, and they realize that this is going to happen, what is that going to do to the incentives to take this work and to stay on the island? Professor?

Dr. JOHNSON. I think that any young person who has the ability to leave will leave, and they will find a good job at a higher wage and better opportunities in the 50 states.

Mr. CARTWRIGHT. So, it is an even bet that this is a proposal that will exacerbate the crisis because of increasing emigration from the island, isn't it?

Dr. JOHNSON. If the Governor opts into it. You do have the safeguard that the Governor would have to own this. I don't know why any governor of Puerto Rico would opt into it, frankly.

Mr. CARTWRIGHT. All right.

Now, Professor Johnson and Mr. Weiss, aside from encouraging young people to leave, what are the other effects that such a low minimum wage on the island would have? What impact might it have on the long-term recovery prospects on the island and its economic stability? Mr. Weiss?

Mr. WEISS. The minimum wage aspect would have to be elected by the Governor. I think the arguments have been clearly stated both by you, Congressman, and by Professor Johnson. The bill in its totality has enormous benefits, though, which in our judgment should stem out-migration if properly implemented.

Mr. CARTWRIGHT. Professor Johnson?

Dr. JOHNSON. I agree with Mr. Weiss.

Mr. CARTWRIGHT. OK. Thank you.

I yield back.

Mr. LAMBORN [presiding]. Thank you.

Representative Duncan.

Mr. DUNCAN. Thank you, Mr. Chairman.

We still have not seen audited financial statements for Puerto Rico, and I think in order to make good decisions here in Congress, we need to see that and understand the ability or inability of Puerto Rico to actually pay.

The Ranking Member used a term earlier, "greedy bond markets," but nobody forced Puerto Rico to borrow this money. Investors took a risk with their hard-earned dollars. It was their money they invested in Puerto Rico. That is not greed, in my opinion. They invested based on a bond that was priced for the risk.

So, let's use terms that are adequate. The Governor of Puerto Rico, I believe, has calculated access to bankruptcy protections far before we started discussing this here in Congress. Are you gentlemen familiar with the Argentina situation?

Argentina has bonds. The Kirchner regime did not want to pay those bonds. They were almost in default. Now we see the Macri government actually come to Wall Street, come to the bondholders, the hedge funds, and actually start renegotiating that debt, and the optimism in Buenos Aires, Argentina, is so strong, you can taste it. Optimism for solvency, access to capital markets for future investment, infrastructure investments, that is the proper way to do it—approach it in a sound, fiscally-responsible manner and renegotiate the debt to come up with a plan.

Mr. WEISS. Congressman.

Mr. DUNCAN. Now, Mr. Miller, Chicago's school system. Your firm invested, last month, $725 million in bonds with an 8.5 percent yield. Does Chicago's school system have access to Chapter 9 bankruptcy courts?

Mr. MILLER. They do not at this time.

Mr. DUNCAN. They do not. And I think that actually reflected on the yield that your investors were looking for. I have trouble comparing the Chicago situation where they do not have access to any bankruptcy protections or whatnot, and the Puerto Rico situation where they do not have access to bankruptcy, but this bill would actually give them some access to some bankruptcy provisions, section 1129 cramdown provisions concern me greatly.

I believe that we are going down a slippery slope here, because states do not have access to bankruptcy protection to this point and under Chapter 9, but I believe that there are many in Congress that would love to see states do that.

I come—my accent may give it away—I come from a southern state. We generally are fiscally responsible in southern states. We do not saddle our citizens with unsustainable entitlement obligations. We do not take on debt. In fact, South Carolina has a balanced budget requirement in our Constitution. We cannot borrow money like that. And if we do borrow money, we have to be able to pay that back. We cannot incur debt after debt.

But what you see in Illinois, California, and New York, they all adopt absurd governing principles of spend, spend, spend, and they pass the political responsibility to another authority. So, I do not want to allow states to be able to access bankruptcy.

Municipal government and other government entities, they are different than private entities. They do not have to fork over capital or hard assets to their creditors when they file Chapter 9.

So, let me just end with this. It is time somebody takes some fiscal responsibility here. I have trouble sitting in the halls of the U.S. Congress when our Nation is $19 trillion in debt on balance sheet, $100 trillion–$150 trillion in debt in off-balance sheet liabilities that the American taxpayers are going to be responsible for, and we are discussing how to tell Puerto Rico how to manage their debt and their fiscal affairs. I really have trouble with that.

Mr. Chairman, I don't really have any questions for the witnesses, and I will yield back.

Mr. LAMBORN. Mr. Weiss, did you have a comment?

Mr. WEISS. Congressman, just with respect to Argentina, two comments. One, it has taken 15 years to resolve, and throughout that period of time, Argentina has been sidelined from markets. Two, Puerto Rico is not Argentina. It is part of the United States.

We have a choice today between a disorderly process, which will ultimately result in a direct transfer of taxpayer funds in the form of a bailout and this is the——

Mr. DUNCAN. Reclaiming my time, I don't have an objection to a control board or an oversight board that will hold Puerto Rico accountable and can renegotiate the debt, not cramdown the debt, not seek bankruptcy type protections.

I think we could do a lot better than what we have done with this bill, but I yield back.

Mr. LAMBORN. OK. Thank you.

Representative Polis.

Mr. POLIS. Thank you, Mr. Chairman.

I appreciate the committee moving forward on legislation to address the devastating debt crisis in one of our territories, Puerto Rico, which serves to remind me how the territory status is neither in the interest of our country nor Puerto Ricans. It is my distinct hope that Puerto Ricans will decide to apply for statehood soon and that we give that application favorable consideration promptly, should that be what the Puerto Rican people choose. Otherwise, we will be back here again in the Natural Resources Committee, where we would never be if this was a state, talking about something that we would never talk about if it was a state, and I think that we should have the same treatment that we would have for any other state in our country for Puerto Rico.

Rather than talk about working out the debt, I want to talk about economic growth and how we can get there. I think the only real way out of this, regardless of what we do and whether Congress tinkers or whether the courts tinker, is we need a higher rate of economic growth in Puerto Rico.

There have been some ideas bandied about here. I think it is no coincidence that with the expiration of section 936 tax credit is when the recession began in Puerto Rico. It may very well not be that instrument. I have a number of ideas, as many other colleagues do, about what we need to do to get a higher rate of economic growth in Puerto Rico. I don't think the answer is lowering the minimum wage with labor and mobility. I cannot imagine, you have a young person who is 20 years old, and they can either earn $4.50 or we have places going the other way on minimum wage, $12, $15. So, you cannot have that kind of delta and expect it to contribute to increased employment when you have labor mobility. The last thing we want to do is lure the best and brightest off the island, especially with the cost of the U.S. Treasury of picking up additional health care, dual-eligible Medicare/Medicaid beneficiaries, all of this cost.

We want a vibrant Puerto Rican economy, and I think we need to look at the way we can do that with all the weapons in our arsenal, including tax credits, including manufacturing, looking at the manufacturing economy. My question for Mayor Williams is, can you speak to the need for economic growth as a component to help Puerto Rico work through the issues of debt and financial responsibility, regardless of what comes out of this Chamber?

Mr. WILLIAMS. I think the control board was a powerful inducement for us to rationalize our balance sheet, establish settled expectations, and, on that basis, begin an economic growth program based on looking at our balance sheet. How do we increase our sales tax by increasing retail, increase growth in the downtown? How do we increase our income tax by bringing new residents to the district? I think very powerfully here, as a matter of compromise, I would prefer a stronger control board, because we had a really strong control board in DC, but I recognize that compromises have to be made. And I think, that said, not letting perfect be the enemy of the good, the oversight board here has powerful tools to influence the right strategy toward growth.

I will say one final thing. One of the things that happened in the District was once we had done some severe cost cutting, rationalization of our balance sheet, established faith and credit, particularly with the Congress, we were able to get, similar to other states, a Medicaid match that worked better for us. I would hope that in this instance, as I alluded to in my oral testimony, that part of this rationalization process, establishing expectations process, Puerto Rico will be able to enjoy the same Medicaid relationship with the Federal Government that other states have.

Mr. POLIS. Thank you.

I yield to my colleague, Ms. Velazquez.

Ms. VELAZQUEZ. Thank you for yielding, and I just want to say for the record that I want to thank Chairman Bishop, Ranking Member Grijalva, and the Resident Commissioner for their leadership, as well as Speaker Ryan and our leader, Nancy Pelosi.

In some areas, we are in a much better place than we were 2 weeks ago when the initial draft was made public. The oversight board has improved, but it still needs further improvement. So the ultimate return for Puerto Rico's economy—it is one thing to have the board approve peaceful plans on—but on a whole different matter to have the board approve. It is not working.

But it is a whole different matter to have the board approve laws, regulation, and contracts. This is a degree of micromanagement, and I will put this plainly. It is insulting to the island, which has a long memory of the U.S. military takeover in 1898. The same is true about the fact that today we don't have among the witnesses any representatives from the government of

Puerto Rico, and here we are discussing important legislation that will impact the lives of the people of Puerto Rico.

What we are demonstrating today as a body, the House of Representatives, is that we have absolute power over the people of Puerto Rico.

So, plainly, we have a colony in the Caribbean. No longer do we use the argument that we can showcase Puerto Rico as a democracy that we use when we needed to get in the face of the Cuban Government.

I yield back.

Mr. LAMBORN. Thank you.

Representative Labrador.

Mr. LABRADOR. Thank you, Mr. Chairman.

Thank you, witnesses, for being here today.

As a person born in Puerto Rico, this has hit close to home. I am now the Representative from Idaho, which is very far away from Puerto Rico, but, obviously, I have many memories. I left the island when I was 13. I have many friends and family members, and I am concerned about the crisis that is happening in Puerto Rico, unfortunately, a crisis that is self-imposed. This is not a crisis of the Government of the United States imposing bad policies on the people of Puerto Rico. This is a crisis of the people of Puerto Rico making unfortunate decisions that have led us to this point that we are dealing with it in Natural Resources, and I wish we were not here to deal with this issue.

I just have a few questions, and I am hopeful that this oversight board will take seriously the opportunity to provide Congress and the President with recommendations on what additional steps we can take on economic policy, because the board by itself and restructuring by itself is not sufficient. There are many other things that we need to do to make sure that the people of Puerto Rico can use the best tools.

And as a conservative Republican, I hope those tools are pro-market tools, because we have seen some anti-market tools being used in Puerto Rico for a long time that have led to this crisis.

Mayor Williams, I thank you for being here again. I have always enjoyed your testimony. How does this bill's oversight board differ from the financial control board that was put in place for DC, and how is it similar?

Mr. WILLIAMS. As I have read the bill and understand the architecture and design of the bill, the board here is intended to be much more principally a convener and a facilitator to use its authority as a gateway to debt negotiation and restructuring; to use its authority to approve a budget to drive the right reorganization, the right rationalization of the balance sheet, and the right performance measures in the government. And I think it is a wise balance, given all of the conflicting views.

All that said, the authority in the District was more direct. The board had the authority in the first instance. It would offer the District the opportunity to do a budget, but after the first instance, we had a 1996 budget called "the 1996 budget on second look," and it was really the 1996 budget you don't want to look at, because it was pretty bad. So, the board ended up doing it itself, so——

Mr. LABRADOR. You mentioned that you would actually prefer a stronger control board. Do you think we could make this a stronger control board?

Mr. WILLIAMS. I recognize that this is a process of compromise and what I am saying is: I think that this bill works to achieve its intended purpose. I mean, yes, in an ideal world, I would prefer a stronger authority. For example, I mentioned a CFO. I think it would be great for the island to have a very strong CFO, going forward, who is autonomous and can provide an autonomous revenue estimate for the country.

Mr. LABRADOR. OK. Thank you.

Mr. Miller, a lot has been said over the past few weeks that this bill will have a disastrous impact on the municipal bond market. Are those predictions accurate, and why or why not?

Mr. MILLER. I don't think those predictions are accurate. These concepts have actually been floating around for several months. In addition, the draft itself has been out for a couple of weeks and the municipal bond market has really been recovering ever since 2013. Excluding Puerto Rico, the risk premiums across munis over and above AAA, they continue to narrow ever since 2013, and in addition, the consistency of investor inflows into muni bond mutual funds, particularly those with less Puerto Rican exposure, the consistency of those inflows has been striking since 2013, with over $60 billion put in.

Mr. LABRADOR. If we pass this bill, will the municipalities in my state, in Idaho, will they have a more difficult time issuing bonds than they have in the past?

Mr. MILLER. No, I don't think so.

Mr. LABRADOR. Will the state of Idaho or any other state have a more difficult time issuing bonds?

Mr. MILLER. No.

Mr. LABRADOR. No. Thank you.

Professor Kent, does this bill set a precedent that will allow states to declare bankruptcy?

Mr. KENT. I don't think it does. There would be very, very serious constitutional difficulties, probably insurmountable, with something that looks like this bill here as applied to the states. There would be problems with the 10th Amendment. There would be problems with sovereign immunity. There would be problems with the so-called contracts clause of the Constitution. No is the short answer.

Mr. LABRADOR. Is this bill constitutional that we are discussing today?

Mr. KENT. I do think it is, yes.

Mr. LABRADOR. OK.

And, Mr. Kirpalani, when we are talking about this debt, there have been some groups that have been calling this Super Chapter 9. Why is this not, or why is it Super Chapter 9? Why isn't it Super Chapter 9?

Mr. KIRPALANI. Right. Thank you, Congressman. The big problem with Super Chapter 9 or Chapter 9 is who controls the restructuring process. If the elected officials are controlling the restructuring process, there is a potential for problem and disappointed results. Here, it is the board that controls it, the board that formulates the plan, and the board that negotiates with the creditors. That is the critical difference.

Mr. LABRADOR. Thank you.

I yield back.

Mr. LAMBORN. Representative Costa.

Mr. COSTA. Thank you very much, Mr. Chairman, members of the committee.

It seems to me that we are engaged in a process here in which there is some precedent when we look at Detroit and we look at New York and we look at other examples over the years in which similar entities have found themselves in this situation for whatever reasons. So I would like to ask questions to Mr. Weiss and Mr. Miller as it relates to the timeline.

But it seems to me, before we get there, in terms of this process, this legislation we are trying to put together, there are three areas that are still being worked on: one is the jurisdiction of this oversight board; two, is the makeup of the board; and, three, is a host of miscellaneous items that have been mentioned, whether it be minimum wage, overtime, the ultimate impacts on the Island of Vieques, which I have been to there. And that is going to be, I believe, at some point in time, the subject of a negotiation, as this legislation already has become.

But let me go to the former mayor here, because you have your own experience and multiple hats that you have worn. Under the category of lessons learned, what would you suggest to us as this legislation is being formed, realizing that, at the end of the day, we are not going to all be satisfied with all of the aspects, but do you think it finds the sort of necessary compromise to get the job done on behalf of the people of Puerto Rico?

Mr. WILLIAMS. Well, in Washington, DC, I think we had our first access to the credit markets for short-term debt in 1996. And I came in in the fall of 1995. There was downsizing that had taken place. We had taken control, under the oversight board, of the financial operations of the District, so I was able to establish credit. It seemed harsh and it seemed severe, but we established faith and credit. We were able to access the markets.

One lesson I think is, in my humble opinion, I don't think you are really helping anyone by trying to be, "too nice." I think it is better to provide the medicine, provide the therapy, and get underway as quickly as possible to establish the expectations, get the economic growth program underway, get access to the markets underway. That is one lesson.

The second lesson that I think is very important and should not be underestimated is, when people talk about budgets, they often talk about conception of the budget, formulation of the budget. But as we have seen in many different levels of government from this level on down, budget execution is crucially important. So, the execution of a budget and a financial plan is just as important as its conception, and I would pay attention to that in the program here.

Mr. COSTA. All right. I want to get to my other questions. But think more about that, and I think if you provided that in the form of a letter to the committee, that would be helpful. By your comments, I assume that the 14-year example in Argentina is not an option in terms of how we go forward.

Mr. Weiss, the legislation has changed. There are modifications that have been made. What additional changes would you like to see in either the jurisdiction of the oversight board or the makeup of the board, all these miscellaneous issues, and please be quick?

Mr. WEISS. We are getting close to a point where there is a potential for a bipartisan solution.

Mr. COSTA. Well, there has to be. Without a bipartisan agreement, there is no agreement.

Mr. WEISS. And without an agreement, there is a collapse in Puerto Rico.

Mr. COSTA. So, for the timelines for that purpose, how quickly do you think we need to get there on this bipartisan agreement?

Mr. WEISS. As soon as this hearing ends, we are going to sit with the Chairman and his staff. We will work through all of our technical edits on this draft, the substantive issues I enumerated in my testimony, and we have to get this done.

Mr. COSTA. We have passed one deadline on April 6. Isn't that correct? Then we have another deadline approaching on May 1, on the $2 billion payment. Then is July 1. So we have several deadlines that are looming.

Mr. WEISS. The time to act is now. We are past every deadline.

Mr. COSTA. OK.

And, Mr. Miller, do you care to confirm, aye or nay.

Mr. MILLER. I agree. The May 1 payment is significant and the July 1 payment is even more significant.

Mr. COSTA. So are those the three buckets, roughly, that we have to find this consensus here sooner rather than later?

Mr. WEISS. Technical items, restructuring workability, and the other items you mentioned. We can get there if there is a will.

Mr. COSTA. Clearly. And without a bipartisan agreement, we have no bill.

Mr. WEISS. Yes.

Mr. COSTA. So it seems like we know where the challenges are as it relates to the jurisdiction, as it relates to the makeup. There are a host of miscellaneous issues that the Representative from Puerto Rico has outlined, and I think we have to come to an agreement sooner than later. We are not going to get everything we want.

Thank you. My time has expired.

Mr. GRAVES [presiding]. The gentleman from California, Mr. LaMalfa, is recognized for 5 minutes.

Mr. LAMALFA. Thank you, Chairman Graves.

Mr. Kirpalani, your clients, my understanding, are GoldenTree Asset Management, Merced Capital, Tilden Park Capital Management, and the Whitebox Advisors. Is that correct?

Mr. KIRPALANI. That is correct, Congressman, in addition to some individuals, yes, sir.

Mr. LAMALFA. When did your clients buy most of their COFINA bonds? Was it before or after 2014?

Mr. KIRPALANI. Congressman, unfortunately, I don't know when they acquired debt. We have represented original owners of COFINA debt, and we continue to do so. And we represent some that have acquired them in the secondary market from people who could not afford to hold onto them.

Mr. LaMALFA. So it is fair to say most of those bonds were bought after it was well known that Puerto Rico was distressed and bought them for less than original investors had paid for them?

Mr. KIRPALANI. I honestly cannot comment as to when exactly they bought them. I would assume that it is a mix: it is probably some who bought initially; some who bought when the debt was at 90, 80, 70. I honestly don't know.

Mr. LaMALFA. So you think it is a mixture. Not all recent purchases——

Mr. KIRPALANI. That is correct. Absolutely right.

Mr. LaMALFA. OK. So these are hedge funds. They regularly seek out situations where, especially post-2014, they are looking to invest in a situation where there is trouble?

Mr. KIRPALANI. These particular clients that I am representing I have actually not seen very active in the hedge fund space. I have never represented them before. There are certain hedge funds, some who have bought up GO bonds in particular, who are looking to try to have an event-driven strategy to capitalize on returns.

Your colleague earlier talked about Argentina. Argentina was held up for 15 years, and the hedge funds that bought Argentine debt actually made 38 percent return for over an 8-year period of time. And some of those funds are actively campaigning now here so that Congress does not act, and they are just hoping that there is no progress, and they will use their litigation tools to try to achieve a result like that.

My clients actually are supportive of responsible legislation. We think that the key point here is that there is a good control board in place and that it respects the rule of law. If we could change anything, we would actually give greater deference to the judicial system in Puerto Rico. For issues of property rights and constitutional rights, to Ms. Velazquez' point earlier, we should defer to the autonomy and sovereignty of Puerto Rico and uphold their laws too.

Mr. LaMALFA. OK. That sounds good.

Now, some of these bonds are not due for quite a few years, a decade or maybe even two decades. But my understanding is that you have been asking the Commonwealth of Puerto Rico to start repaying sooner than they would have under the original agreement. So, with Puerto Rico being in such a cash-stressed situation, why would these particular investments, especially the more late-arriving investments, go to the head of the line for repayment with that much stress?

Mr. KIRPALANI. That is a terrific question, Congressman. Let me try to explain in a very short period of time here. Investors who bought COFINA senior bonds, this was the original safe bond that was introduced when the economy actually collapsed in 2006 in Puerto Rico. There were long-term investors, as you said, for 40 years, 30-something or 40 years, and the protection they had was if there is a default, they would get paid ahead of any bonds that came later. So there is a big swath of subordinated bonds, contractually junior bonds, somewhat called junkier bonds, that came later. So, the only thing that we were saying is: We will reduce the overall payment requirements. We will give back $19.5 billion over the next 35 years to the people of Puerto Rico, and the only thing we ask is respect our contract rights—that is all—and that we get paid before the juniors. But some of them actually will get paid later than maturity, absolutely.

Mr. LaMALFA. For those that would go ahead of their contracted time, though, isn't that kind of stepping out of line? Wouldn't that be kind of a windfall for those?

Mr. KIRPALANI. No, sir, because contractually upon a default, everything is accelerated and it is due immediately. So what we would do is actually forbear, take no payments at all for a year, and then have payments for the next 5 years and slowly inch back up to what the government of Puerto Rico has said they could actually afford. So the only issue, really, between us and the Commonwealth of Puerto Rico are the holdup creditors, who are the junior bondholders who will not go along. That is the problem.

Mr. LaMALFA. OK. Thank you for your answers. I will yield back, Mr. Chairman.

Mr. GRAVES. Mr. Clay is recognized for 5 minutes.

Mr. CLAY. Thank you, Mr. Chairman.

Professor Johnson, one of the areas of concern for me is: How do we best protect pensioners and retirees who, no fault of their own, stand to be hurt by severe reductions in pension benefits? Have you given that much consideration?

Dr. JOHNSON. It is a very difficult issue, Congressman. So, as you know, people who live in Puerto Rico pay payroll taxes, and they do receive Social Security. So there is a Federal dimension. But there are also government people who work for the government who receive government pensions. And those pensions are, without question, under pressure. And the pension fund, I believe, is out of cash or very nearly out of cash.

I think that what you say in legislation is that there has to be a sustainable fiscal plan. To Ms. Velazquez' point, I believe that what you have here is a governor with the right to design a plan making decisions, including about what happens to pensions. That plan has to be consistent with what the board regards to be sustainable, but that level of decision, I believe, if you were to pass this legislation, would still reside with the Governor and the legislature of Puerto Rico.

I don't have an easy answer. There are no easy answers. But that is a decision that will be made by the elected officials of Puerto Rico.

Mr. CLAY. Thank you.

Mr. Weiss, the proposed legislation does a delicate dance with the creditors of the island nation. In its current form, will this provide the solution, or is there more work to do there?

Mr. WEISS. Congressman, we believe that we can get there if the good spirit of cooperation on technical items which need to be remedied remains in place and we work quickly and diligently, we believe that we can get to a workable solution. I highlighted three elements in my oral testimony where I think substantial work needs to be done first. There will be a host of other technical issues. But as Congresswoman Velazquez pointed out, we have made a lot of progress.

This is the mayor's term. This is a wise balance. It is tough for the people of Puerto Rico. It is tough for their creditors, some of them. But in the aggregate, it is going to produce the best overall results in our judgment, properly constructed for the people and for the investors.

Mr. CLAY. Thank you.

Mr. Chairman, at this time, I will yield to my friend and colleague from New York, Ms. Velazquez.

Ms. VELAZQUEZ. Thank you.

I thank the gentleman for yielding.

Mr. Johnson, members here are concerned and troubled by the fact that, yes, in Puerto Rico, they have made bad decisions fiscally. They have spent too much. But I would like to ask you—workers in Puerto Rico pay the same payroll taxes as those living in the mainland, yet they receive fewer benefits than those who live in the United States. Do you think that is fair?

Dr. JOHNSON. No, Congresswoman, I don't think it is fair. In a previous hearing, I testified that my recommendation would be to move Puerto Rico toward the same fiscal relationship with the Federal Government that the 50 states have. I think that would be fair. That would be reasonable. You could separate it from the issue of statehood, although, obviously, it comes up in the context of statehood.

And, specifically, I wish that you were addressing the earned income tax credit in this legislation because that is one salient point that actually people on the right and the left generally agree on is a sensible program, and Puerto Rico, people who live and work in Puerto Rico do not have access to that, as you know.

Ms. VELAZQUEZ. Well, the fact of the matter is that this legislation that we have before us lacks any economic growth policy. And yes, that will be one area that will benefit greatly the people of Puerto Rico.

Mr. Weiss, in your testimony, you stated, and I quote, "The process for entering restructuring should not require a supermajority vote of the board. A minority of the board should not have veto power at the critical juncture when all other options have been exhausted."

Given your comments, is it your view that requiring five board members to vote affirmatively to approve Puerto Rico's entrance to judicial restructuring is an insurmountable hurdle, in fact, denying Puerto Rico restructuring authority?

Mr. WEISS. Congresswoman, it is one of the three elements I highlighted in my oral testimony. I absolutely stand behind the words that I used. But I also expect that it will be among the issues where we can make progress with the committee and with the Chairman and his staff.

Ms. VELAZQUEZ. OK.

Thank you, Mr. Chairman. I yield back.

Mr. GRAVES. Mr. Westerman is recognized for 5 minutes.

Mr. WESTERMAN. Thank you, Mr. Chairman.

And thank you to the panel for being here today.

As unpleasant and as unfortunate as this debt issue is in Puerto Rico, I am actually glad that we are here in Congress talking about debt, and I hope that we will have more serious discussions about debt. I say that based on the fact that if you look at the debt per capita in Puerto Rico, $115 billion over roughly 3.5 million people, that is just under $33,000 per person. If you look at the debt here in United States, $19.2 trillion over 323 million people, that is over $59,000 per person.

We have a debt per capita 81 percent higher than the territory of Puerto Rico. This may be the classic example of worrying more about the plank in our own eye than the speck in our neighbor's eye. That said, I think we can learn from history. Any of us who have made an investment have probably read the small print that says: Past performance is not an indicator of future performance.

My state of Arkansas has a statistic that I am not very proud of. We were the last state to default on our debt. It happened in 1933. It happened after the state had invested heavily in bonds for infrastructure, a couple of natural disasters, crash of the stock market, and the state found itself in a very precarious situation. When we talk about bankruptcy, I think to the common person, our state was bankrupt, but we did not have Chapter 9 bankruptcy protection.

One historian wrote that we were flat broke. The State Treasurer said at one point in time the balance in the state budget was $4.92. Arkansas suffered through that. They took a substantial hit to their bond rating. It was actually 1949 before the state ever issued another bond. But through that, we also put better fiscal policies in place. We had a balanced budget act that was passed. I was serving in my state legislature in 2011 when many states were having fiscal issues. Our state was actually cutting taxes and had a surplus budget because of the pain that we had suffered many years ago and the reforms that we had put in place.

Mr. Weiss, other than the fact that Puerto Rico has not fixed their problem, what is the emphasis for the Federal Government to interject itself into the Puerto Rican debt issue? And I remind you that it is the Federal Government that is 81 percent per capita more in debt than the government that we are trying to help.

Mr. WEISS. The Federal Government borrows on a 10-year basis at 1.75 percent. Puerto Rico is borrowing in excess of 12 percent. In fact, it is not borrowing at all right now because it is shut out. We have three interests: Number one, we believe that the safety and economic well-being of the 3.5 million Americans in Puerto Rico is at stake. Essential services today are being curtailed. Hospitals are being shut and out-migration has accelerated to the extent that 2.5 percent of the Americans in Puerto Rico are now coming into the mainland every year.

We are inextricably bound to Puerto Rico. How they got there is not a topic of today's discussion. There is a long history of mismanagement that extends back decades. But the complexity and extent of this debt crisis is such that it falls on Congress to act in order to set Puerto Rico back on the right path.

Mr. WESTERMAN. Mr. Kent, even if a future Congress tried to use this legislation to establish precedent for a Chapter 9 protection for states and potentially violate the Constitution in doing so, would that Congress still not have to pass legislation? And is there not precedent that establishes no Chapter 9 protection allowed for sovereign states? That question has been asked many ways. It is another attempt.

Mr. KENT. Certainly, Congress would have to authorize it. And as I said before, I think the constitutional difficulties are so severe that it is hard for me to imagine how it could possibly be constitutional with regard to the states. There is contracts clause, there are sovereign immunity issues, and then there are also issues with 10th Amendment and state sovereignty being invaded. So, I just don't see how it could happen.

Mr. WESTERMAN. Mr. Miller, I may have time to get this question out there. Would this legislation cause a ripple effect in the bond market?

Mr. MILLER. No, I think the opposite. I think it would be a calming effect on the bond market.

Mr. WESTERMAN. And the opposite of that, if nothing is done, would it cause a ripple in the bond market?

Mr. MILLER. The risk is higher if nothing gets done.

Mr. WESTERMAN. OK.

Thank you, Mr. Chairman.

Mr. GRAVES. Thank you.

I recognize myself for 5 minutes.

Mr. Kirpalani, I heard folks talking earlier about ads that are being run in various districts. Could you give your opinion on what you think the outcome of those who are funding those ads is, what their objective is?

Mr. KIRPALANI. Sure. Thank you, sir.

To be perfectly honest, just to start with, this is my first experience with Washington and with this whole political process. I didn't even know——

Mr. GRAVES. I would urge you to leave.

Mr. KIRPALANI. I didn't even know that you could do that kind of thing, place ads in the newspapers in Members' home districts when they are at home on recess with their families. I think it is really horrible.

I think that the real goal here is, if you really dissect, which I have been doing over the last 10 months or so, what the motivations are, the folks that are putting the ads, they bought New York-governed GO bonds issued by Puerto Rico. So just take a step back and think about that. The sovereign of Puerto Rico, territorially sovereign of Puerto Rico, issues bonds, but the creditors insisted—and these are creditors who insisted that the minimum entry to participate in that offering is $100,000 a pop. This is not your individual retail customer. OK. These are sophisticated, well-heeled institutions. And they said: We know how to make gambles. Our gamble is this Congress in a bipartisan way will never act. So, therefore, let's put New York law to govern the Puerto Rico general obligation bonds so that when Puerto Rico collapses, which it has done, and Puerto Rico issues a debt moratorium law, which it has done, we will ride free. So the only way that that debt could also participate in an overall restructuring process is if the U.S. Congress acts. They are just hoping that does not happen.

Mr. GRAVES. Do you think that they would also prefer some type of bailout from Congress or from the Federal taxpayers?

Mr. KIRPALANI. They are just spinning absolute fiction. That is what they are doing. There is no bailout concept here. There is nothing in the bill that suggests a bailout. It is, frankly, just the opposite. It is the only way to rationalize the resources that are available to repay creditors in a timely way. I am also representing a couple of individuals: Barry, from Minnesota, who is a retiree from New York City, a former public worker; as well as Pepin from San Juan, who is also retired but, unfortunately, now has to restart working at a dry cleaning business.

These folks want to hold on to their investments. They cannot afford to sell them at the depressed prices. They just need to get repaid, and they are worried very, very much about their financial future. And this type of responsible legislation gives them encouragement.

Mr. GRAVES. Thank you.

Mr. Weiss, thank you for returning. Your testimony in both instances has been very educational. I know you have been asked this question in some form previously, but could you explain what you view as being the alternatives right now that Congress has in order to address the crisis in Puerto Rico right now?

Mr. WEISS. Thank you, Congressman.

On the one hand, it is a cascading series of defaults, mounting litigation. The constitutionally-protected debt that is due in July cannot be paid. The moratorium which has been enacted in Puerto Rico will apply in each subsequent repayment instance. In our judgment, chaos will ensue, and the economy will face another lost decade with accelerated out-migration.

Our alternative to that, which involves pain for all sides, but, again, is this wise balance, is to put in place independent fiscal oversight and a restructuring set of tools, both incentives for voluntary negotiations and a fallback in the event that those fail. This is, by far, the best outcome for the people of Puerto Rico, for markets as a whole, as a colleague has attested, and, ultimately, will provide the best recovery for creditors taken as a whole.

Mr. GRAVES. Mr. Weiss, would you see no action by the Congress as increasing the chances of liability for taxpayers or decreasing?

Mr. WEISS. There is an element of inevitability around that question. This is the alternative to a bailout.

Mr. GRAVES. Thank you.

One last point I want to make and I know time is about to run out. Look, I don't want to get into a political or partisan battle in this hearing. I appreciate the cooperation everyone has had. There has been a bit of a focus on minimum wage, and I just want to make note that, in 2013, there was unanimous action by this Congress to ensure or to prevent the increase in minimum wage in territories in the United States, again, unanimously passed, signed by this President. I understand that there are challenging conditions, but I have concerns with imposing the minimum wage standard for the most developed country in the world upon some territories that may not have similar conditions. I just want to make note, and I am looking forward to continuing to work with all of you on establishing the best policy.

I will now recognize Mr. Hice for 5 minutes.

Mr. HICE. Thank you, Mr. Chairman.

Professor Kent, you made the comment earlier, and I just want to clarify, that in your opinion this bill is constitutional, correct?

Mr. KENT. Yes, I think Congress has power under the territorial clause.

Mr. HICE. Is there any constitutional precedent where this has, or something similar has, taken place in the past with another territory?

Mr. KENT. I am not aware of one, but there are, as I said, identical clauses. The problem here would be if the bankruptcy clause is said to apply and require uniformity. But like I said, there is precedent that the other uniformity clauses in the Constitution do not apply to Puerto Rico and similarly situated territories. So, I don't think there will be that problem. Congress could act in a way that either territory, across all the territories or specific to Puerto Rico, I think, without a constitutional problem here.

Mr. HICE. OK. We are also being told, just to carry this line of thought a little further, that what is happening and what is being proposed here, constitutionally, with Puerto Rico does not set a precedent for states or cities. Out of curiosity, does anyone know, of the other U.S. territories, are any of them in any financial problem?

Mr. MILLER. The territory that probably has the best reception and the narrowest risk premium in the marketplace is Guam, and the balanced budget and most stable economy. Some concerns about Virgin Islands, some delayed audits, but not anywhere near this kind of magnitude.

Mr. HICE. OK. But there is potential that we could be facing this with some other territories at some point?

Mr. WEISS. Puerto Rico is multiples more stressed than any other territory.

Mr. HICE. I understand that. But my question is, are we going to be running down this path? Once we set a precedent here in Puerto Rico, are we going to be running down this at some point elsewhere?

Mr. WEISS. The U.S. Virgin Islands ran a referendum as to the viability of a CFO, not even a control board. And by memory—and I ask to verify this with you afterwards—I believe two-thirds or three-quarters of the citizens voted against in that referendum.

Mr. HICE. OK. Let me go on a little bit further, and, Professor Kent, I will stay with you, I think, for this question. Municipal bondholders who have a particular interest in Puerto Rico probably are in every district represented in this committee and in Congress, for that matter, and probably senior citizens are most affected by that. This bill clearly has Congress changing the rules after they have purchased an investment. Is it your belief, is it your testimony, that Congress has the constitutional authority to change the rules after the fact on municipal bondholders or anyone else?

Mr. KENT. Yes, the Constitution protects contracts against states changing them, but it does not have a similar protection for the Federal Government. That is because the Federal Government has the power over bankruptcies. But as I said here, with regard to territories, Congress has an alternate basis, and it could enact bankruptcy legislation under the territorial clause.

Mr. HICE. I understand that case here. But you are saying constitutionally Congress has the authorization to come in after the fact and change the rules of the game of investors?

Mr. KENT. Well, as I understand the process, that is what happens with bankruptcy.

Mr. HICE. I understand the process. I am asking constitutionally.

Mr. KENT. Yes.

Mr. HICE. I would like an answer from you in writing, if you can, where in the Constitution that would be found.

Let he hit my final thought here. Yes or no, Mr. Weiss. Let me just ask you this: Is it problematic at all that the oversight board has no one representing the bond market on the oversight?

Mr. WEISS. The composition of the oversight board has not been determined.

And with respect to your other question, the 2014 prospectus that Mr. Kirpalani described expressly provided that there could be a change in law——

Mr. HICE. OK. Last question. Thank you.

Mayor, you have had experience with this, both on the board in DC and as mayor. The tax incentives, there have been changes recently. All have resulted in declining jobs. What tax incentives need to take place? And I would really like to hear from Mr. Johnson as well on this, your suggestion as to what tax incentives need to be in place.

Mr. WILLIAMS. Again, I think the board can help rationalize the financial performance plan on which you can build economic incentives. I don't know particularly which. But by assuring the markets that there is execution in the government and settled expectations on the performance of the government, you can then begin to build economic investment.

Mr. HICE. Could I get your answer in writing here, Mr. Johnson, if you would, please? If I could have that, I would appreciate it.

Thank you. I yield back.

Mr. GRAVES. Mrs. Radewagen is recognized for 5 minutes.

Mrs. RADEWAGEN. Thank you, Mr. Chairman.

While Congress and certainly this committee understand the need for this legislation, I do believe that it might not go far enough in providing the tools Puerto Rico needs to recover from their current fiscal crisis.

There are many good measures in the bill that will do a great deal to resolve the issue, but there are also other things that can be done—and some may have mentioned this already, but I wanted to go on record—such as putting the territories on the same footing as the states when it comes to the earned income tax credit, the child tax credit, and removing the caps on Medicaid.

Just quickly, anybody on the panel, can any of you explain to me why these proposals should not be part of this bill?

Dr. JOHNSON. Well, Congresswoman, I had previously testified in a hearing of a subcommittee of this committee exactly in favor of those changes. I can send you that testimony if you don't have it readily available.

I do recognize that this is a political process here, and I recognize that not everything that everybody wants can be in this particular piece of legislation, but I think the Congress will have to come back to these issues or the closer related issues in the near future because encouraging and stimulating growth in Puerto Rico is going to remain an important priority. This bill is a first step, can become a first step, but I think you are going to have to do more.

Mrs. RADEWAGEN. Thank you.

Mr. WILLIAMS. I would agree with that, for the record.

Mrs. RADEWAGEN. Thank you.

And, last, I notice that in the final draft, the name of the board has been changed from the Puerto Rico Oversight Board to the Territorial Oversight Board. That actually makes Americans far more nervous. While this may seem trivial, I am concerned with this renaming and its implications as well as some of the language in sections 303 and 401, which essentially gives Congress carte blanche power over the territories.

In your opinion, would the language contained in this bill grant Congress unlimited powers with regard to the other territories?

Mr. WEISS. With respect to the other territories, there is an opt-in feature such that the other territories would have to choose through their own democratic process to elect the powers which were described in the article to which you refer.

Mrs. RADEWAGEN. Thank you, Mr. Chairman. I yield back.

Mr. GRAVES. I am going to recognize Mr. Pierluisi for a brief closure.

Mr. PIERLUISI. Thank you, Chairman.

I would like to clarify a couple of things for the record. Part of this overspending is definitely the result of mismanagement. I admit it. And it is embarrassing. But part of it is lack of adequate Federal funding in key areas such as the health of the American citizens living in Puerto Rico.

Let me just give you an example. Under the Medicaid program, Puerto Rico is entitled to get about $350 million a year. With ObamaCare in place, the additional funding given by the Affordable Care Act, Puerto Rico is getting about $1.2 billion a year from the Federal Government to take care of the medically indigent in Puerto Rico, American citizens.

Oregon, which has a similar population to Puerto Rico, gets $5 billion a year. You don't need to be an economist or a CPA to know the huge difference between $1.2 billion a year and $5 billion a year. Wouldn't that help Puerto Rico's fiscal condition? That is just an example.

My other comment has to do with growth. We are all about growth. Puerto Rico is not going to grow when its government is failing, when its government has become an impediment to growth, when its government owes contractors from the private sector over $2 billion.

We need to stabilize the government so that Puerto Rico grows. And talking about growth, I have to remind everybody here that the last two territories that became states, Hawaii and Alaska, within 10 years each doubled their economy. So if we want growth, let's change Puerto Rico's status.

Thank you, Mr. Chairman.

Mr. GRAVES. Ranking Member.

Mr. GRIJALVA. Thank you, Mr. Chairman.

I want to thank the witnesses. I appreciate very much the testimony. We are getting down to the point that if a true bipartisan legislation is to appear, it needs to appear immediately.

I echo Mr. Weiss' points on areas I think need to be worked on for the sake of a bipartisan agreement.

I also want to say that this is an alternative to a bailout, and I really appreciated the question. People said, "Oh, this is a bailout; this is unconstitutional; this skirts bankruptcy laws," and all that, which through this testimony has proven not to be the case.

Having said that, though, this is an alternative to a bailout because, in the short term, if Congress truly understands both its fiduciary and, indeed, its moral responsibility to our fellow citizens in Puerto Rico, we have to do something, because something will be done, and the humanitarian crisis spurred by this economic and fiscal crisis cannot be tolerated.

I hope, for all the stakeholders in this, that a very important effort is done to satisfy a bipartisan piece of legislation and that the narrow interests in this question are ignored and the majority interest is taken care of, and that is the people of Puerto Rico.

I want to thank you, Mr. Chairman, for the hearing, and I look forward to a product that we can all comfortably support on the Floor.

With that, I yield back, and thank you.

Mr. GRAVES. I thank the witnesses for their valued testimony and the Members for their questions.

The members of the committee may have some additional questions for the witnesses, and I will ask that you would respond to those in writing. Under Committee Rule 4(h), the hearing record will be open for 10 days for these responses.

If there is no further business, without objection, the committee stands adjourned.

[Whereupon, at 12:51 p.m., the committee was adjourned.]

[ADDITIONAL MATERIALS SUBMITTED FOR THE RECORD]

PREPARED STATEMENT OF THE HON. STACEY E. PLASKETT, A DELEGATE IN CONGRESS FROM THE U.S. VIRGIN ISLANDS

Thank you Chairman Bishop and Ranking Member Grijalva for holding this hearing to consider H.R. 4900, an act to establish an Oversight Board to assist the Government of Puerto Rico, including instrumentalities for managing its public finances, and for other purposes.

The people of the United States Virgin Islands and the other territories are aware of the fact that for over a year now, there have been discussions in Washington around the concerns facing Puerto Rico and their continuing debt crisis.

While I am generally supportive of Congress acting to resolve an issue affecting one of the territories, I am concerned that a large number of the discussions, thus far, have been focused solely around the fear of the collapse of Puerto Rican bonds, instead of the underlying issues that led to the debt crisis.

In October 2015, the White House issued a roadmap to recovery for not only Puerto Rico, but for the other insular territories that were also in need. In that proposed roadmap, the White House requested that Congress address several areas other than bankruptcy, including:

- Expanding and lifting the overall cap on Medicaid;
- Increasing tax relief for residents through the Earned Income Tax Credit and Child Tax Credit;
- And increasing access to credit opportunities.

These were all areas of focus not just for Puerto Rico but for Guam, American Samoa, Northern Mariana, and the Virgin Islands.

The Governor of the U.S. Virgin Islands, my fellow Democratic House Members, leaders in Puerto Rico, and myself all agreed that these options were an important start to helping us create real economic growth for our territory.

After several months of pushing for a package to help all territories create economic opportunity, it became evident that the relief coming out of this Congress would be focused solely on bankruptcy protection.

I believe this is a mistake. I believe this Congress and this legislation should focus on putting in place the mechanisms needed to ensure that our economies could actually grow.

H.R. 4900 mentions nothing about Medicaid, or any other tax relief, nor does it provide any other recommended economic growth options. It will review Puerto Rico's pension system and deals primarily with the mechanism for Puerto Rico's restructuring of its debt.

This bill does so by creating an Oversight Board, a Board with very broad powers over the Puerto Rican government. Rather, it allows a stay on payments, while the Board reviews the Puerto Rican finances, and that Board will ultimately determine if Puerto Rico can restructure.

However, what is more alarming, is the fact that PROMESA also contains a provision, which states that the other territories may also have oversight boards, if the local Legislature and Governor request it from Congress.

I cannot support this bill creates a Territory Financial and Oversight Management. Any language that implies Federal oversight, as to how we govern ourselves, even if it implies that local support is required, is not acceptable.

I am concerned not only about over-reach by the Federal Government, but by the chilling message this may send to our own creditors and investors countering the confidence that our Governor and legislature have created over a number of years of hard work.

I believe the Territorial Financial Oversight and Management Board provision in H.R. 4900 to be detrimental to the advancement of our local government. It provides a tool for financial restructuring instead of providing resources for the other territories to avoid a debt crisis and economic growth for all territories. The territories did not ask for an oversight board. Therefore, the passage of this bill should not hinge on the inclusion of the other territories.

I will also continue to press for the development and creation of true economic growth opportunities, like those I referenced earlier.

Thank You.

THE ASSOCIATED GENERAL CONTRACTORS OF AMERICA,
PUERTO RICO CHAPTER,
SAN JUAN, PUERTO RICO

April 11, 2016

Hon. ROB BISHOP, *Chairman,*
House Committee on Natural Resources,
1324 Longworth House Office Building,
Washington, DC 20515.

Re: Puerto Rico Oversight, Management and Economic Stability Act ("PROMESA")

Dear Chairman Bishop:

The Puerto Rico Chapter of the Washington, D.C. based Association of General Contractors of America ("AGC-PR") wishes to thank you, members of the Committee and staff for the work and effort related to Puerto Rico, its current crisis and the potential solutions. In connection therewith, we hereby formally express particular support for a fiscal control board for Puerto Rico to address the current fiscal and economic crisis. We also express our strong support for Title V of PROMESA[1] (as it relates to infrastructure investment and economic development), which undeniably is at the center of the current crisis and the key to any sustainable solution.

Any federal structure that may be legislated to help Puerto Rico address the current crisis must not only address the issue of debt but—at the same time and possibly with greater emphasis and priority—must ensure sustainable economic growth, development and certainty. This includes contractual certainty (rule of law) to enable small, medium and large investors and business concerns to invest, perform and receive payments therefor. Without this, any debt or fiscal restructuring will only postpone the inevitable, to the detriment of all U.S. citizens still residing on the Island as well as those who have invested in Puerto Rico instruments.

It is widely known that our infrastructure, whether energy,[2] water and sewer,[3] solid waste management,[4] roads and bridges[5] and low income housing,[6] is in need of replacement, modernization or new construction. The Committee is well aware that Puerto Rico's permitting process poses significant challenges for the Island's general competitiveness—resulting in long and inefficient practices that generate uncertainty and discourage investment. Permitting reform is needed and should also contemplate government restructuring in order to achieve sustainable efficiencies and government transparency. Recent studies commissioned by the current administration expressly recognize the need to address permitting issues in order to improve and achieve sustainable economic growth.[7] Puerto Rico has the necessary statutory and regulatory structure to reform permitting. Any final version of PROMESA (Title V) should ensure that Puerto Rico immediately undertakes (implements and maintains) the permitting reforms needed to ensure economic growth, investment, jobs and infrastructure capable of providing citizens quality services as well as protecting the environment and human health.

The AGC-PR represents 80% of the overall economic activity in construction and has 300 members with diverse professional backgrounds and experience covering construction industry areas that include but are not limited to energy, roads, water and sewer, housing, tourism, and facilities for the manufacture of pharmaceutical and other products as well as technology and research and development.

Our historic role and impact on the local economy was very significant as compared with today.

---

[1] The discussion draft released by the House Committee on Natural Resources on March 29, 2016.

[2] The power generation fleet of the Puerto Rico Electric Power Authority is very aged and inefficient (median generating plant age is 44 years vs. an industry average of 18 years).

[3] Potable water reservoir capacity around most of the island is severely impaired given a lack of maintenance; water and sewer treatment and distribution facilities require significant capital investments (for federal environmental compliance, efficiency and related factors) for which the Puerto Rico Aqueduct and Sewer Authority does not have the funds or even the current ability to access the capital markets.

[4] As recent as March 2016, EPA informed that 20 of the 27 landfills in operation on the Island are not in compliance with local or federal regulations that protect human health and the environment—and as such, pose a direct threat to surface and ground-waters (potential or actual drinking water sources), soils and air, in and around communities near these noncompliant facilities.

[5] The Puerto Rico Highway & Transportation Authority lacks the funds for the construction of 1new roads and/or bridges or their adequate maintenance.

[6] [_____]

[7] The Kruger Report states: 26. **A lot can be done to lighten the burden of doing business, which is particularly important when reforms are aiming to move the economy in new directions.** To date, the term business-friendly in Puerto Rico has referred to efforts to offset high input costs with tax breaks and subsidies. As input costs are brought down, the focus should shift to ensuring a level playing field and greater ease of doing business, including permits for new businesses. This is always an on-going task but a start could be made by addressing the three weakest areas identified by the World Bank: the difficulty in registering property, in paying taxes, and in obtaining construction permits . . . (Emphasis ours). *See* Puerto Rico—A Way Forward, Anne O. Krueger, Ranjit Teja, and Andrew Wolfe, June 29, 2015, http://www.bgfpr.com/documents/puertoricoawayforward.pdf; *See* Page 27 of the Puerto Rico Fiscal and Economic Growth Plan prepared by the Working Group for the Fiscal and Economic Recovery of Puerto Rico Pursuant to Executive Order 2015–022, September 9, 2015; http://www.bgfpr.com/documents/PuertoRicoFiscalandEconomicGrowthPlan9.9.15.pdf.

Following are some telling data points:

Area	Historic	Current
Jobs	90,000	20,000
Gross National Product	10%	3%
Investment	$6B	$2B

The local construction industry's situation is evidently aggravated by the current fiscal crisis, as by the Administration's delay in paying government contractors for services rendered.[8] Furthermore, very recent government actions like the highly controversial enactment of Act 21–2016 (Moratorium Act) last week and ongoing discussions by local government officials about bankruptcy, defaults and the ability to expropriate private property and services without proper procedures has only added to the general uncertainty of citizens and the business community—confirming the investing community's perception that Puerto Rico, a U.S. Commonwealth, is a high risk investment jurisdiction.

PROMESA will undoubtedly provide Puerto Rico with the necessary structure, and immediate credibility, to quickly begin addressing the most fundamental budgeting, cost-control, efficiency and transparency requirements of a fair and equitable government. Similarly, Title V will help implement and maintain the regulatory conditions necessary to facilitate critical infrastructure projects, related investments and economic and job growth. We trust and support that the final version of PROMESA and Title V be designed to ensure that Puerto Rico can retake the path of a supportive government while allowing the private sector to jumpstart economic development, create jobs and provide opportunity to thousands of citizen on the Island. We urgently need a climate of credibility, transparency and certainty that maximizes Puerto Rico's ability to overcome the current crisis.

Again, thank you and the Committee for its work and efforts related to Puerto Rico. We stand ready and available to assist in any way the Committee deems relevant and appropriate.

Sincerely,

ENG. NEYSSA VARELA,
President.

———

Hon. ROB BISHOP, *Chairman,*
House Committee on Natural Resources,
Washington, DC 20515.

Dear Chairman Bishop:

Respectfully request a personal interview with you in your Washington D.C. office, at some time between April 12–15, 2016.

I am Jose Olmos, Republican and leader within the Veteran and Military community in Puerto Rico. After 27 yrs of service in the Army Reserve and Army National Guard, as a Citizen Soldier I retired as Lieutenant Colonel in 2011. For many years I have been active in Puerto Rico educating the political leadership on the importance of the contributions made by our citizens to national security. At present I am running for office to become the 1st State Representative in Puerto Rico political history that strongly and without limitation supports the Veteran/Military Community and the Caribbean Security of the United States.

Under your leadership as Chairman of the House Natural Resources Committee you intend to present a bill whose objective is to "To establish an Oversight Board to assist the Government of Puerto Rico, including instrumentalities, in managing its public finances, and for other purposes." This proposed bill has been in preparation by your committee for several months and has received input from many political, commercial and industrial leaders of Puerto Rico.

---

[8] It was unofficially stated (by the Secretary of Treasury) last week that the total debt due to Government service providers has reached the amount of over $2.2 Billion. With respect to PR-AGC members, as of March 2016 the Puerto Rico Aqueduct and Sewer Authority alone owes multiple members over $160 Million, with no near term capacity to pay these amounts.

But one community that has not been heard is the Military Community of Puerto Rico, composed of 150,000 veterans and over 50,000 service members in all the military components of the nation. I am sure that you have not received any input or comments from the perspective of national security or considered the 117 years of loyal military service to the nation by the American Citizens of Puerto Rico. My intend is to move you to consider that any Bill to "assist the Government of Puerto Rico, in managing its public finances" is incomplete if you don't consider the Blood, Sweat and Tears spilled by the American Citizens of Puerto Rico in the defense of the nation.

The solution of Puerto Rico economic problems is not only a question of financial loss; it is also a question of facing the real challenge of giving equal political right to Puerto Rico. The Bill that you propose will only place a temporary bandage to the festering wound of a colonial relationship.

Next July 25, we commemorate 118 years since the U.S. Armed forces INVADED Puerto Rico, following the orders of a REPUBLICAN President and supported by a REPUBLICAN Congress. Our ancestors received those troops as liberators and welcomed the American flag in 1898 because they believed it, and we still believe today that it is a symbol of democracy and justice. Since then we have struggled to be responsible, loyal and patriotic citizens. But today, although we enjoy great material wealth our political liberties are more restricted than when we were under the colonial rule of Spain. Why you may ask? Then as today our final destiny as Puerto Ricans is subject to the whims of a Central Government who is unwilling to make up its mind. The main difference is that the USA Congress created a facade to hide its control of the island. I think that the Spaniards were more truthful in their actions.

I want to meet with you and hear from you, how will you explain to the thousands of Veterans and Military Personnel/Citizens from Puerto Rico that they are equal on the battlefield but not in the Voting Booth. How will you explain to the military widows and orphans that the sacrifice of their parents is worthless and diminished by the economic interest of Wall Street? How will you justify the continued inequality to thousands of parents who lost their sons in distant battlefields for the defense of an ungrateful nation?

The economic crisis of Puerto Rico needs urgent attention but the Blood, Sweat and Tears of our soldiers has to be considered in the solution. Any solution can't be at the expense of passing the final solution of the island political status to another generation. The time to act is now.

Thank you for the opportunity and look forward to a sincere face-to-face conversation.

Sincerely,

JOSE O. OLMOS

P.S. Below are some facts related to the military contribution of the American Citizens of Puerto Rico.

It is important for you to become aware that PUERTO RICO IS THE CARIBBEAN BORDER OF THE USA. The Caribbean border is as important as the Mexican Border and currently is wide open leaving 3.5 million American Citizens in the Island at risk of terrorism, narcotics and the enemies of our Great Nation that move their ships freely within the area. It is time that the Caribbean Border receives the attention it merits to be secured.

1. Puerto Rico National Guard plus Reserves contribute more Citizens Soldiers to national Defense than 22 States.

2. There are approximately 150,000 veterans in the island plus their family members.

3. There are more than 50,000 Puerto Rican soldiers in Active Duty in all the branches of the armed forces.

4. Puerto Ricans have carried the burden of defending the nation in equal terms with our continental brother in arms since 1899.

5. WE ARE EQUAL IN THE BATTLEFIELD BUT NOT IN THE VOTING BOOTH.

6. We don't want to continue a relation with the USA as a colonial dependency.

7. WE HAVE FOUGHT IN EVERY WAR FOR 117 YRS. The liberty, security and prosperity that the USA enjoys today were paid in part with the BLOOD, SWEAT AND TEARS of disenfranchised citizen soldiers of Puerto Rico.

8. The Puerto Rico National Guard and Reserve Components are the best-trained, lead and equipped force in the Caribbean. After 15 yrs actively contributing and mobilizing for the GWOT their combat and operational experience has no comparison within the military and security units of other Caribbean nations. The National Guard and Reserves should lead the efforts to secure the Caribbean Border by becoming the trainers and on site force that works with partner nations in the area.

————

OUTDOOR ALLIANCE

April 12, 2016

Hon. ROB BISHOP, *Chairman*,
Hon. RAÚL GRIJALVA, *Ranking Member*,
House Committee on Natural Resources,
Longworth House Office Building,
Washington, DC 20515.

Re: Puerto Rico Oversight, Management and Economic Stability Act discussion draft

Dear Chairman Bishop and Ranking Member Grijalva:

We write to express our serious concerns with certain aspects of the "Puerto Rico Oversight, Management and Economic Stability Act" discussion draft, which the House Natural Resources Committee will consider this week. In particular, we are concerned by the proposed transfer of thousands of acres from the Vieques National Wildlife Refuge to the government of Puerto Rico, which we believe sets a dangerous precedent by facilitating the potential privatization of protected public lands.

Outdoor Alliance is a coalition of seven member-based organizations representing the human powered outdoor recreation community. The coalition includes Access Fund, American Canoe Association, American Whitewater, International Mountain Bicycling Association, Winter Wildlands Alliance, the Mountaineers, and the American Alpine Club and represents the interests of the millions of Americans who climb, paddle, mountain bike, and backcountry ski and snowshoe on our nation's public lands, waters, and snowscapes. Our members are deeply committed to the protection and responsible stewardship of our country's public lands.

Outdoor Alliance recognizes that targeted and limited land exchanges or small-scale transfers are an appropriate land management tool under certain circumstances. However, a proposal directed toward the privatization and development of protected public lands as part of a potential solution to a governmental entity's financial problems is wrongheaded. Public lands—particularly those given additional protections for their ecological or recreational values—are a trust that should be retained in public ownership and managed for benefits in perpetuity, not in response to temporary financial exigencies.

We ask that the Committee carefully consider the dangerous precedent set by this proposed transfer and demonstrate its commitment to America's public lands by removing this problematic provision.

Best regards,

ADAM CRAMER,
Executive Director.

PUERTO RICO BUILDER'S ASSOCIATION

April 12, 2016

Hon. ROB BISHOP, *Chairman,*
Hon. RAÚL GRIJALVA, *Ranking Member,*
House Committee on Natural Resources,
Longworth House Office Building,
Washington, DC 20515.

Dear Chairman Bishop and Ranking Member Grijalva:

At this time, we bring to your attention, the Discussion Draft, submitted by the Committee you lead, to establish an "Oversight Board to assist the Government of Puerto Rico."

As you well know, through the National Association of Home Builders (NAHB), we represent the construction and housing industries across our Nation, which includes our Puerto Rico Chapter. As such, we are committed to give an informed input to your Committee on this subject, having discussed and studied this serious matter with our colleagues and fellow companies of our Puerto Rico Chapter.

In light of this preliminary analysis, we provide the following conclusions or recommendations, on this matter:

a. A federally-appointed Fiscal Control Board is an important and necessary step to tackle Puerto Rico deep fiscal crisis on the short-term.

b. We believe a good-faith and upfront negotiation should be done between the Government of Puerto Rico, its creditors and any Fiscal Control Board established by Congress.

c. This Fiscal Control Board should be established, in conjunction with a clearly defined mechanism for the restructuring of Puerto Rico's non-guaranteed debt, that is to say, every portion of the debt owed by public corporations, not guaranteed as a general obligation under the local Constitution or any other guaranteed agreement or legislative act.

d. This Fiscal Control Board must be complemented with a strong economic redevelopment plan, to stimulate the Puerto Rico economy. No fiscal control effort will make sense without an economic recovery. Included herein is a document outlining suggestions on actions needed to secure economic prosperity.

e. Every federal piece of legislation, adopted to attain the aforementioned goals, should be approved with adequate instruments to secure complete accountability and transparency from the Government of Puerto Rico, including but not limited to a thorough disclosure of Puerto Rico's updated financial state, current debt and assets.

f. Legislation should include measures that improve the investment and economic climate of the Commonwealth of Puerto Rico. There will be no fiscal relief or assistance to the local government without an economic recovery.

As you can conclude from the elements described above, the Association and our Puerto Rico local Chapter, have a business-oriented standpoint, geared toward a balanced and reasonable solution to Puerto Rico's fiscal challenges, without any partisan consideration.

Also, this balance can only be accomplished by a combination of a federally-appointed Board that gives stability and certainty to Puerto Rico's fiscal scenario, a restructuring of the non-guaranteed debt and a strategic, coherent and federally-sponsored economic redevelopment plan.

Regarding this last component, we believe some short and medium-term economic measures should be enacted to stimulate the Real-Estate and Construction Sector of Puerto Rico's economy.

We will give the highest priority to the analysis of any other recommendation we deem appropriate to submit to your Committee concerning this matter. Finally, we thank you in advance for your consideration and analysis you can give to our statements and proposals.

Best regards,

ARCH. RICARDO ALVAREZ-DÍAZ, AIA, NCARB,
President.

JUBILEE USA NETWORK,
WASHINGTON, DC

April 13, 2016

Hon. ROB BISHOP, *Chairman*,
House Committee on Natural Resources,
1324 Longworth House Office Building,
Washington, DC 20515.

Dear Mr. Chairman:

On behalf of Jubilee USA we want to thank you for your leadership, as well as that of Speaker Ryan and Representative Duffy to move forward a solution for the financial crisis affecting 3.5 million Americans.

Jubilee USA's founders and members include 550 Churches and Synagogues, and groups like the U.S. Conference of Catholic Bishops, The Episcopal Church, American Jewish World Service and Islamic Relief USA. Our religious coalition works closely with a coalition in Puerto Rico that represents 95% of the population and Catholic, Evangelical and Pentecostal religious groups. San Juan's Catholic Archbishop, Methodist Bishop, Lutheran Bishop and head of the island's Bible Society are calling for solutions that protect their people from further austerity policies.

Mr. Chairman, on behalf of Jubilee USA we need to affirm that there can be no economic growth in Puerto Rico until the debt is brought back to sustainable levels.

Congress must adopt a solution that promotes budget transparency, reduces child poverty and ensures strong provisions to restructure the debt in a manner that is timely, comprehensive and orderly.

As you know, we've organized religious communities across our great nation and on the island of Puerto Rico to pray for you as you move legislation forward. As you begin your deliberations, I wanted to share the thoughts of the island's religious leaders.

Puerto Rico's Catholic Archbishop, Roberto Octavio González Nieves, O.F.M., encourages Congress to "work together to find a solution to the crisis that respects the rights and dignity of all sides. I invite the people of Puerto Rico and all people of faith around the world to join me and pray for the U.S. Congress as they consider action around Puerto Rico. We also must pray for Puerto Rico's leaders and creditors to work together to find a solution to the crisis that protects the rights and dignity of all sides. We pray that any solution seeks to reduce child poverty on the island and invest in our people. We pray that solutions respect Puerto Rico's democracy. Finally we pray that any solutions will ensure that the debt is brought to payable levels, without further sacrifice to our social services."

Reverend Heriberto Martínez, the head of Puerto Rico's Bible Society said, "It is urgent that leaders of our country and creditors can sit together at the table of dialogue and fellowship to find a responsible solution that does not sacrifice our people, already going to a very difficult situation. Our creditors should recognize that above any further consideration should be the well-being of human beings. The well-being of my brother and sister is and should be our main and highest priority."

We look forward to continuing to work with you throughout this legislative process.

Gratefully,

ERIC LeCOMPTE,
Executive Director.

April 14, 2016

Hon. PAUL RYAN,
Hon. NANCY PELOSI,
U.S. House of Representatives,
Washington, DC 20515.

Hon. MITCH McCONNELL,
Hon. HARRY REID,
U.S. Senate,
Washington, DC 20510.

Dear Speaker Ryan, Majority Leader McConnell, Democratic Leader Pelosi and Minority Leader Reid:

State and local governments have a keen interest in federal legislative efforts to bring fiscal reforms to Puerto Rico. For example, an essential component of any federal fiscal reform package to aid Puerto Rico must be that such a plan is specific to the territory and does not contain provisions that could be construed as having application to U.S. state and local governments. We will aggressively work to oppose federal legislation that contains such extraneous provisions, including the *Public Employee Pension Transparency Act* (PEPTA). Such legislative provisions would needlessly expand the scope beyond Puerto Rico, impose unnecessary and undue regulatory burdens on U.S. state and local governments and threaten the federal tax exemption on municipal bond interest.

State and local governments of all sizes access the tax-exempt bond market to provide essential infrastructure. Through the tax-exemption, the federalist system of reciprocal immunity continues to provide critical support for the federal, state and local partnership to develop and maintain essential infrastructure. State and local governments provide three-quarters of the total investment in infrastructure in the United States,[1] and tax-exempt bonds are the primary financing tool used by state and local governments and authorities nationwide to satisfy these infrastructure needs. State and local governments issue approximately 11,600 bonds a year totaling roughly $300 billion on average. This has allowed state and local governments to finance more than $3.5 trillion in infrastructure investment over the last decade through the capital markets.

We support legislative efforts tailored specifically to Puerto Rico that will establish an orderly process to immediately initiate steps to restore fiscal order to the island and maintain critical services to the citizens of Puerto Rico. Such a process is preferable to a less orderly plan that pits Puerto Rico against its creditors in lengthy negotiations while government services to the citizens of Puerto Rico deteriorate and a humanitarian crisis ensues. The latter of which could expose U.S. state and local governments to unyielding and inaccurate speculation about the likelihood of their defaulting on their debt obligations, and drive news media and federal policy makers to draw false comparisons between Puerto Rico, which is a U.S. territory, and mainland state and local governments.

This kind of conjecture ignores that fact that bankruptcy, while headline-grabbing, is rare and is not an option for most localities. State and local governments recognize that the general obligation pledge is widely relied upon by municipal entities across the country to access the capital markets, and place significant value on upholding this pledge. Historically, municipal bonds have had a significantly lower average cumulative default rates than global corporates overall and by like rating category.

For example, between 1970 and 2013, the average 10-year default rate for Moody's Aaa-rated municipal bonds was zero compared to a 0.49 percent default rate for Moody's Aaa-rate corporate bonds.[2] Furthermore, over the last five years, during which state and local governments struggled to recover from the Great

---

[1] Public Spending on Transportation and Water Infrastructure, 1956 to 2014: Congressional Budget Office, 2015.
[2] Moody's Investor Service—U.S. Municipal Bond Defaults and Recoveries, 1970–2013, May 7, 2014.

Recession, rated state and local GO defaults were remarkably low at 0.005 percent.[3] In the double-A rating category to which the majority of municipal ratings were assigned, average cumulative default rates are much lower for municipals than for corporates with the same double-A symbol.[4] There has been only one state that has defaulted on its debt in the past century, and in that case bondholders ultimately were paid in full.

Thank you for your consideration of these comments.

Sincerely,

Matthew D. Chase, Exec. Director,
National Association of Counties

Clarence Anthony, Exec. Director,
National League of Cities

Tom Cochran, CEO/Exec. Director,
U.S. Conference of Mayors

Jeffrey L. Esser, Exec. Director/CEO,
Government Finance Officers
Association

Robert J. O'Neill, Executive Director,
International City/County
Management Association

———

COUNCIL FOR CITIZENS AGAINST GOVERNMENT WASTE (CCAGW),
WASHINGTON, DC

April 19, 2016

U.S. House of Representatives,
Washington, DC 20515.

Dear Representative:

On behalf of the more than one million members and supporters of the Council for Citizens Against Government Waste (CCAGW), I strongly urge you to support H.R. 4900, the Puerto Rico Oversight, Management, and Economic Stability Act (PROMESA). This legislation creates an essential mechanism to thwart a taxpayer bailout of Puerto Rico's fiscal failures.

On April 12, 2016, Rep. Sean Duffy (R-Wis.) introduced PROMESA, which would establish an oversight board to assist the government of Puerto Rico, including instrumentalities, to manage public finances. The legislation provides reforms that will allow the territory to fulfill its debt obligations responsibly and efficiently. It will also help the citizens of Puerto Rico prosper from a growing economy. The bill is designed to address problems related solely to Puerto Rico and will neither have any impact on existing bankruptcy provisions that govern states or their municipalities.

The structure of the oversight board is based on the precedent established in 1996, when Congress set up a financial control board to oversee the fiscal affairs of the government of the District of Columbia as well as the control board set up for New York City in 1975. PROMESA is not a bailout, despite misleading advertisements to the contrary. Indeed, without the enactment of H.R. 4900, taxpayers will inevitably be forced to bailout Puerto Rico in the near future.

I urge you to vote in favor of PROMESA in order to create a fiscal oversight board for Puerto Rico and ensure that taxpayers are not liable for any defaults on the territory's debt obligations. All votes pertaining to PROMESA will be among those considered in CCAGW's *2016 Congressional Ratings*.

Sincerely,

TOM SCHATZ

---

[3] Municipal Market Analytics (MMA).

[4] Moody's Investor Service, https://www.moodys.com/research/Moodys-Municipal-bond-defaults-remain-low-in-number-but-new_PR_298814.

SIFMA ASSET MANAGEMENT GROUP

April 21, 2016

Hon. ROB BISHOP, *Chairman,*
Hon. RAÚL GRIJALVA, *Ranking Member,*
House Committee on Natural Resources,
1324 Longworth House Office Building,
Washington, DC 20515.

Re: Congressional Action to Address the Puerto Rico Municipal Market and Contagion

Dear Chairman Bishop and Ranking Member Grijalva:

On behalf of the Asset Management Group ("AMG") of the Securities Industry and Financial Markets Association ("SIFMA"), I am writing to support Congress' efforts to create a limited and targeted framework to address Puerto Rico's fiscal crisis through H.R. 4900, the Puerto Rico Oversight, Management, and Economic Stability Act ("PROMESA").

SIFMA AMG is the voice for the buy-side within the securities industry and broader financial markets, which serves millions of individual and institutional investors as they save for retirement, education, emergencies, and other investment needs and goals. SIFMA AMG's members represent U.S. asset management firms whose combined assets under management exceed $30 trillion. The clients of AMG member firms include, among others, registered investment companies, separate accounts, ERISA plans, and state and local government pension funds. Some SIFMA AMG members have more exposure to the debt of the Commonwealth of Puerto Rico and its instrumentalities than others, but all care deeply about ensuring that Puerto Rico's financial situation is addressed appropriately, without negatively affecting the broader municipal bond market.

Puerto Rico's financial crisis is unique and complex, and it therefore requires a unique solution. We believe that the combination of the establishment of a federal oversight board and a restructuring framework that is based on the Territorial Clause of the U.S. Constitution, will create a comprehensive solution to aid Puerto Rico's economic recovery, improve the island's financial position, and prevent Puerto Rico's situation from leading to higher permanent borrowing costs for other municipal issuers.

In particular, SIFMA AMG supports the creation of a federal oversight board with broad powers to enforce and monitor fiscal discipline. We believe this is a practical way to address the current crisis in Puerto Rico. We support Congressional efforts to ensure that the oversight board will treat creditors fairly and protect valid and legal liens during the restructuring process. SIFMA AMG also supports the inclusion of a provision that allows creditors an opportunity to vote on any debt restructuring plans.

While many details about this legislation remain in flux, we believe the municipal market would and should welcome appropriate Congressional action to address the financial crisis in Puerto Rico. We urge Congress to act quickly before the situation worsens. Thank you for your leadership on this issue. We look forward to partnering with Congress as it works toward final passage of this legislation.

Sincerely,

KENNETH E. BENTSEN,
President and CEO.

PIMCO Blog

Congress Needs to Act on Puerto Rico's Debt Crisis, and 'PROMESA' Could Work

Authors: David Hammer, Sean McCarthy, and Libby Cantrill
Published: April 26, 2016

Diverse interests have emerged seeking to derail a bill aimed at a satisfactory resolution to Puerto Rico's debt crisis.

The U.S. House Natural Resources Committee (HNRC) is considering H.R. 4900, entitled the Puerto Rico Oversight, Management, and Economic Stability Act, or PROMESA, which means promise in Spanish. A critical component of the bill is creation of a federal oversight board with broad powers over Puerto Rico's fiscal and budgetary affairs. The seven members of the oversight board would be appointed by the U.S. president, but chosen from lists of qualified candidates offered by various parties.

Some critics have protested the potential infringement on Puerto Rico's sovereignty, while others want assurances the island territory or investors will not get a "bailout." (PIMCO currently manages more than $40 billion of municipal investments issued by U.S. cities, counties and states. PIMCO portfolios do not hold any exposure to bonds from the Commonwealth of Puerto Rico or its various governmental entities.)

In our view, PROMESA represents a responsible framework for managing the unavoidable restructuring of Puerto Rico's debt and other liabilities. We expect no contagion to the broader municipal market from PROMESA. More specifically, PROMESA will not trigger higher borrowing costs for states or municipalities.

Some are worried the federal government might take over a state's finances in a similar manner; yet there are no convincing arguments because the Constitution protects the sovereignty of the states. Again, this bill wouldn't create such a precedent. PROMESA is possible because the Constitution explicitly allows Congress to set all laws on U.S. territories, which have fewer rights than states.

In addition, it would be incorrect to classify PROMESA as a "bailout." No incremental federal tax dollars are allocated to the Territory under the bill. In fact, if this legislation does not advance, the probability of future federal tax dollars flowing to the Territory or bondholders may actually increase.

The failure of U.S. Congress to address the complex fiscal and debt crisis in Puerto Rico is a greater risk to the $3.5 trillion tax-exempt municipal market. It is essential to enact a stay on litigation to provide a fiscal control board with an appropriate amount of time to reach a sensible solution. Without a stay, creditor litigation on individual liens is likely to ensue. The outcomes of these decisions have the potential to set confusing precedents for not just holders of general obligation debt, but for other portions of the municipal market, including holders of essential service revenue bonds that constitute the majority of outstanding municipal debt.

Time matters. At this point, it appears that the 1 May deadline to address the worsening situation in Puerto Rico will not be met, and Puerto Rican issuers will likely miss some of the $470 million debt service due on that date. Some hope that the missed payments will add pressure on policymakers to act, but given the disagreement between the parties (and within the Republican Party), it appears that the crisis will have to get worse before it is tackled by Congress. An even larger debt service payment looms on 1 July.

Accordingly, we urge Congress to continue moving PROMESA forward. A successful resolution to the unique crisis in Puerto Rico can only be achieved with a strong federal oversight board empowered to both enforce fiscal discipline and adjust the Territory's public debt in a fair and equitable manner designed to achieve debt sustainability. We believe PROMESA will achieve these objectives.

———

[LIST OF DOCUMENTS SUBMITTED FOR THE RECORD RETAINED IN THE COMMITTEE'S OFFICIAL FILES]

—Numerous letters from the Puerto Rico Citizen Coalition in favor of the Federal Fiscal Control Board.

○